AF531702

THE POST-SOVIET CONDITION
Chingiz Aitmatov in the '90s

RASHMI DORAISWAMY

ACADEMY OF THIRD WORLD STUDIES
Jamia Millia Islamia
New Delhi

AAKAR BOOKS

THE POST-SOVIET CONDITION
Chingiz Aitmatov in the '90s
Rashmi Doraiswamy

First Published, 2005

Published by
AAKAR BOOKS
28-E, Pocket-IV, Mayur Vihar Phase-I, Delhi-110 091
Phone : 011-2279 5505 Telefax : 011-2279 5641
E-mail : aakarb@del2.vsnl.net.in

Typeset at
Arpit Printographers

Printed in India on behalf of M/s Aakar Books by
Phones : 09350809192, 011-22825424
arpitprinto@yahoo.com

CONTENTS

Acknowledgements 7

I. Chingiz Aitmatov in Soviet and Post-Soviet Times 9

II. Resurrection of Memory: *The White Cloud of Genghis Khan* 17

III. Ethics in the Time of Dystopia: *The Mark of Cassandra* 23

IV. Local Destinations: *A Night of Remembrances about Socrates...* 46

V. Dialogues on the Passing of a Century: Chingiz Aitmatov's Conversations With Daisaku Ikeda and Mukhtar Shakhanov 53

VI. Changing Contexts, Shifting Stands: Interviews and Essays of the '90s 67

VII. In Transit Through Systems 81

Bibliography 99

Index 105

ACKNOWLEDGEMENTS

I am very grateful to the following people and institutions for help received while writing this monograph:

- The Director, Professor Mushirul Hasan, for encouragement to work on Central Asian culture at the Academy of Third World Studies;
- Dr. Ranjana Saxena (Delhi University), for long discussions on Russian and Soviet literature and for generously sharing contemporary critical works from Russia as well as Aitmatov's *Tavro Kassandry* with me;
- Professor Varyam Singh (Jawaharlal Nehru University), for lending me Aitmatov's recent book, *Plach Okhotnika Nad Propastiyu*;
- The Russian State Library (formerly known as the Lenin Library) in Moscow, for access to books by and on Chingiz Aitmatov;
- Sitora Alieva, for making arrangements for my stay in Moscow to work in the Russian State Library;
- The library, Academy of Third World Studies;
- The library, Jawaharlal Nehru University;
- My parents, brother, husband and children for their constant support.

I

CHINGIZ AITMATOV IN SOVIET AND POST-SOVIET TIMES

Writer, playwright, translator, essayist, Chingiz Aitmatov was born in an ail in Talas Valley, Kyrgyzstan in 1928. He grew up listening to Kirgiz epics and myths from his grandmother and aunt. His father was an active member of the Communist party, who became a victim of Stalinist purges. In 1942 he left school because his mother could not afford to send all her children to school and rejoined it after the war. He became secretary of the village Soviet at fourteen. He worked in the ail as a taxman and a clerk for tractor drivers harvesting wheat. After the Second World War, he went back to school. He then joined the veterinary training college and graduated from the Kirgiz High School of Agriculture with distinction. He worked as a livestock specialist till 1956 doing translations and writing articles. Although he had published several short stories in the early '50s, he enrolled for the Higher Literary Courses in Moscow in 1956. He then became an editor at *Literary Kirghizstan* and later, *Pravda* correspondent from his republic. It was *Jamilia* (1958) that made him famous in the Soviet Union. It was translated into French by Louis Aragon who called it the most beautiful love story in the world. Within a decade of starting to write, Aitmatov was known nationally and internationally.

Cultural Icon

Aitmatov has lived through the major political events of XX century Russian history: the socialist transformation of life in Kyrgyzstan in the aftermath of the October Revolution, Stalinism, the II World War, post-war reconstruction, the Thaw, Stagnation, Perestroika and the collapse of the Soviet Union. He is currently Kyrgyzstan's Ambassador Extraordinaire to Benelux, the European Union, NATO and UNESCO and lives in Brussels and Kyrgyzstan. His works have been reprinted many times and translated into many languages. He has received the highest awards in the land, including the Lenin Prize for Literature. The evocative imagery of his works have led to adaptations into films, opera, ballet and plays.

Chingiz Aitmatov has straddled two worlds: the traditional world of the ails and of the modern cities of the Soviet Union. He speaks and writes in both Kirgiz and Russian. These openings onto different realms, energizing Aitmatov's creativity were possible in the great social churning that socialism unleashed. The dialogical interweaving of oral and written traditions was to become a hallmark of his work from *Farewell, Gulsary!* onwards. If, on the one hand, he had access to the wealth of oral literature in his native Kyrgyzstan, he was familiar with the best of world literature, on the other. Aitmatov states that "... I am of the firm opinion that the influence of the Russian classics and that of contemporary literature in these regions has been decisive. Russian history was such that its literature became the expression of the people's spirit. It took a lot upon itself. And for that reason there existed a special kind of reverence towards literature, towards the written word, as also towards the writer. Close contact with European literature enabled it to simultaneously amalgamate that experience and create a totally unique literature capable of depicting a whole range of complexities. So when other literatures entered its orbit they too were strongly influenced by Russian literature. ... This is one of the main factors responsible for the resurgence, and applies even more so to the Asiatic Republics. .... Our acquaintance with Russian literature grew side by side with the fact that it also began to serve as a measure of values for us, for it was there, right next to us. All of a sudden we acquired an aesthetic system for evaluating, so to speak, the development of a truly good literature"[1].

Chingiz Aitmatov was thus a product of the socialist transformation of the Soviet Union. A writer who had learnt his political and aesthetic

---

1. 'From the Aiil to the Cosmos', Chingiz Aitmatov interviewed by Kalpana Sahni, Journal of Arts and Ideas, January – June, 1987, p 5.

lessons well at the Institute, he implemented them in his works. His writings are some of the best examples of the tenet 'socialist in content, national in form'. He went on to critically evaluate political and aesthetic positions. Although he was highly awarded and widely showcased by the Soviet State as proof of the cultural success of socialism in the Central Asian Republics, he could not escape the rigors of censorship. He was asked to rewrite the ending of *The White Steamship*, because it was too pessimistic. Critiquing the state or its functionaries and policies was not easy while living in such proximity to it. Yet, Aitmatov found a way of moving into the chronotope of legends and myths to create parallel worlds that held up mirrors to this world. It is this intertwining of two separate modes of narration that makes it difficult to compartmentalize works like *Mother's Field* or *Farewell, Gulsary!* in the accepted categories of 'war prose' or 'village prose'. The interweaving is itself a sign of the fluid mix of identities that encompass Kyrgyzstan and Russia, oral and written narratives, realist sensibility and the pre-realist. His works were a testimony to his mastery over the mode of realism, worked out by Russian writers, combined with an assertive dose of national traditions.

Periodization of Work

Aitmatov's works can be classified into three broad phases. This categorization is based on the way in which he views conflict in the plot. While the first short stories, written in the '50s, had the protagonists commit violence on themselves and those dear to them, due to a weakness in their own characters, there is a shift in the works of the '60s. The larger social context, which lies beyond the immediate transformative power of the individual, becomes the cause of this violence. This period begins definitively with his novella, *Mother's Field* (1963). In works such as *Farewell, Gulsary!* and *White Steamship*, the violence is unleashed either by war, or by an insensitive party bureaucracy, that does not comprehend the finer details of the day-to-day life of people on the periphery. This problematic is made more dense by the introduction of fables and parables into the plot of the novellas, that accentuate the sense of loss and pain in the main narrative. Chingiz Aitmatov's first novel, *And the Day Lasts longer than a Century* (1980), marks the beginning of the third phase. Science-fiction is incorporated into the realist–parable framework of plot construction. It also clearly pits the individual against the State. Aitmatov's work of the '90s develops further, by linking the corruption of party officials in the Soviet system to Stalin and Stalinist methods of governance, in which the coercion of masses play a crucial role.

Chingiz Aitmatov has written short stories, long stories/novellas (*povesti*), novels, and co-authored plays. His work graph, in fact, moves from short stories, to novellas, to novels. While he continues to write in other forms and modes simultaneously, he seems to have progressed to ever larger literary forms. His style evolves as he moves to larger forms. His first work is a short story, *Dzuiyo, the Newsboy* (1952). His first novella is published in 1958: *Jamilia.* He continues to publish short stories like *Red Apple* (1963) and *Meeting With the Son* (1964). He publishes his first novel *And the Day Lasts Longer Than a Century* in 1980, nearly twenty-eight years after his first work.

In each of the three periods in Aitmatov's works, there is always a work that stands slightly apart from the set of thematic preoccupations being dealt with. In the first period, it is *Jamilia* (1958). In the second phase, it is *Piebald Dog Running on the Seashore* (1977). The utopic elements of the parables woven into *Farewell, Gulsary!* and *The White Steamship* find expression in the ethnographic realism of *Piebald Dog*. In the third phase, the work that stands apart is *The Mark of Cassandra* (1995), for being a 'global' narrative, set in lands far away from Kyrgyzstan. These works are different, because they elaborate Aitmatov's thematic preoccupations in a given period from a completely different angle. A. Fedotov too, divides his works into three periods, but from a geographical point of view: "The first books gaze down from the heights of the Tien Shan and Pamir mountains on the young motherland Kirgizia. After that the geography of the books extends to the expanses of the Soviet Union – Russia, Kazakhstan, the Far East. In the recent novels you are literally observing the whole planet from a cosmic height. And in addition to this particular kind of realism there is an entry of the fantastic into the plot"[2].

The 'Positive Hero'

There is thus a clear line of development in Aitmatov's work which

2. *Chingiz Aitmatov: Stat'i, Vystupleniya, Esse, Dialogi*, Sobraniye Sochinenij v 7 tomakh, Tom 7, Moskva, 1998, Tom 7, p. 529.

is interesting to examine from the point of view of the canon of socialist realism. The tenet of the positive hero, that was to be found in every socialist realist work, is thus taken up at different levels by Aitmatov who diligently learnt his lessons at the creative writing school. If in the first phase of his work, for the most part, the impulse to negative behaviour (which is not fully within the realm of Evil), is to be found in the protagonist himself, in the later works it is corrupt party officials, craving for the next step on the ladder of power, who carry the mark of Evil on them. In the post-'80s phase of his work, we find that the notion of Evil has shifted to those leaders who coerce at mass levels, very different from the more local injustices unleashed on the protagonists of works of the second period . The positive hero, thus in many of Aitmatov's works, carries the element of tragedy within himself. As against the classical notion of the tragic character who has the one fatal flaw—the Achilles heel in an otherwise noble bearing—within himself, in realist fiction, the impulse to a tragic destiny is generated in the larger social context of which the protagonist is part. In Aitmatov's early work, the element of conflict is dealt with through the character's own failings, but later his vision becomes more complex. While the premise of 'revolutionary historical optimism', another defining tenet of socialist realism is adhered to, there are elements of tragedy that seep in quietly, but firmly into the plots. The tragic vision rests in the impossibility of the full realisation of the 'new socialist human being', in the given socio-political circumstances. 'Revolutionary optimism' is invested in the fact that despite such overwhelmingly adverse circumstances such as war, political intolerance and corruption, the protagonists do manage to retain a sense of dignity and belief in ideals, even in the face of death.

This development of a vision, form and style point to a steady maturing of Aitmatov's work. Halim Kara's view that Aitmatov was a 'captive mind' who tried to widen the circle of literary possibilities according to relaxations in censorship and the State control, is a simplistic and misleading one[3]. Aitmatov, like many other writers of the time, was a 'critical insider', not an oppositional writer, or a dissident. In an interview in 1997 he states:

3. 'Chingiz Aitmatov: A Captive Mind', Halim Kara, Paper presented at the Fourth Annual Central Eurasian Studies Conference, Indiana University, February, 8, 1997.

> "I want to speak about what is close and at the same time painful to me—the individual and the state. Today, civilisation appears to give priority to the individual. But in those days it was understood a little differently. The state and Party interests were given first place. You could debate this only if you were a dissident, and there *were* dissidents. But all writers did not have to be dissidents. Most of us remained at our posts, in our milieu, dealing with real historical situations and atmosphere. We found that our own forms of confrontation—and literature and art—were effective ways of defending our positions.
>
> Literature reached its apogee in these years; it enjoyed immense popularity, played an important role in Soviet society and answered many questions which we could not answer ourselves. In fact, its position was almost sacramental. My own work had its place in this process"[4].

After the collapse of Soviet Union, many writers fell silent, not knowing how to image and figure reality in extreme flux in their works. It is to Aitmatov's credit that he continued to publish, even though he too lived through the crises of form and ideas. In the last leg of the period of perestroika, in 1990, he published *The White Cloud of Genghis Khan*, a novella. In 1993 he published *Dialogues at Ikeda's Campfire*, ruminations on the state of the world with the President of the Soka Gokkai International Buddhist order. 1995 saw the publication of *The Mark of Cassandra*. In 1996, he published two works with the Kazakh writer, diplomat and political activist, Mukhtar Shakhanov: a play, *A Night of Remembrances About Socrates, Or A Judgement on a Self-Seeker With a Stupid Face*, and *The Hunter's Lament Over the Precipice*.

This book analyses Aitmatov's works of the '90s and examines the ways in which they relate to questions of identity and geopolitics in literature. The fall of the Soviet Union left its cataclysmic impact on the cultural sphere. The impact made itself felt in the work of one of the leading writers of the Soviet Union whose literary career was, in fact, fashioned by the dominant political and cultural milieu of the USSR. This study addresses the questions of how Aitmatov coped with the post-Soviet condition in the '90s, how he represented a changed world and how he represented himself. It also attempts to

4. 'The Truth on Mount Fuji', Interview with Chingiz Aitmatov by Latika Padgaonkar, The Pioneer, New Delhi, 11 December, 1997.

place Aitmatov's works of this period in the context of the changing face of realism in Russia and relevant international debates on cultural theory. Although Chingiz Aitmatov's works were widely disseminated and discussed during the Soviet period, his works of the '90s have not received much critical attention in Russia, even though they have been written in Russian. This book[5] critically examines all his works of the last decade of the twentieth century.

Aitmatov's writings manifest in differing ways the 'post-Soviet condition'. The Central Asian Republics did not want to break away from the Soviet Union, when the fall became imminent. The 'post-Soviet condition' for Kyrgyzstan, therefore, was a condition born not of choice. There was a double bind of the need to carve a distinctive Kyrgyz national identity and, at the same time, to integrate the past (Soviet and pre-Soviet) into this new identity. According to Robert

---

5. The chapters that constitute this book have been presented as papers at various national/international seminars and conferences:
   * *Changing Contexts, Shifting Stands: Chingiz Aitmatov in the '90s*, paper presented at the seminar 'Russian Literature, Language and Culture Today', **Ch. Charan Singh University, Meerut**, 8-9 March, 2005;
   * *Dialogues on the Passing of a Century: Chingiz Aitmatov in Conversation with Daisaku Ikeda and Mukhtar Shakhanov*, paper presented at the seminar 'India-Asia Aesthetic Discourse', **IIAS, Shimla**, 23 September, 2004; a shorter version of this paper was presented on 10 December, 2004 at the seminar 'Contemporary Trends in Russian Language and Literature', **Russian Centre for Science and Culture, New Delhi**;
   * *Systemic Transition and the Literary Process: A Case Study of Chingiz Aitmatov*, paper presented at the seminar on 'Systemic Transition in the CIS', **SIS, Jawaharlal Nehru University**, 24 March, 2004;
   * *Mapping Histories, Relocating Identities: Chingiz Aitmatov in the '90s*, paper presented on 9 December, 2003 at the seminar 'Identity and Geopolitics in Central Asia: 1991 – 2003', organized by **ATWS, Jamia Millia Islamia**, 9 - 10 December, 2003;
   * *Ethics in the Time of Dystopia: A Study of Aitmatov's 'The Mark of Cassandra'*, paper presented at the seminar: 'Central Asia – Its Land and People', **Centre for Advanced Study, Aligarh Muslim University**, 8 – 11 April, 2003.

Lowe, "It is impossible to ignore the enormous changes wrought by the Soviets, and improvements in literacy, healthcare and the emancipation of women are still admired. Furthermore, it is impossible to correct the basis of the Soviet nationalities policy that legitimizes Kyrgyzstan's existence. The leadership also remains essentially the same as before independence, and the people have no desire to dismiss the Soviet years entirely. Therefore, unlike the experience in other Central Asian states, a measured acceptance of the immediate past, and not an attempt to erase it, has been a subtle element of the nation-building process. While there has been much discussion of the theoretical need to rewrite history and remove the Soviet/Russian bias, little has been done in practice. Certain dark areas of the past have been illuminated, like the 1916 revolt and the purges of the 1930s, and some historical figures rehabilitated, but not to the same extent as in Uzbekistan and Kazakhstan"[6]. Aitmatov's works of the nineties, in keeping with this dominant trend in the nation-building process, reflect a critique of, as well as an integration of the Soviet past into the Kyrgyz present.

Political independence brought with it a new economic order: socialism was abandoned in favour of market economy. There was also an 'opening out' into globalisation. All these processes were to profoundly affect cultural production. Not only did the material conditions of this production change (there was no longer any state support and censorship), there was also a need for the artist to reposition his/her self ideologically in the new socio-economic and political context. The 'post-Soviet condition' is thus deeply marked by the dismantling of all 'big narratives': of being part of one of the two superpowers of the world, of a 'brotherhood of peoples', of an internationalism, of cultural practice within the limits of the canon of socialist realism. This study analyses the ways in which Chingiz Aitmatov's works of the nineties reflect and refract the paradoxes of this condition.

---

6. 'Nation Building and Identity in the Kyrgyz Republic', Robert Lowe, in *Central Asia: Aspects of Transition*, Tom Everett-Heath (ed.), Routledge Curzon, London 2003, pp. 121-122.

II

RESURRECTION OF MEMORY

The White Cloud of Genghis Khan

Aitmatov calls *The White Cloud of Genghis Khan* a 'novella towards a novel'. This was a part of his first novel, written in 1980, *And the Day Lasts Longer than a Century*, that he had refrained from giving for publication[1]: "Not rarely, in the interests of the work being published 'in full', one had to agree to a lesser evil, so as to not to—speaking in images—overload the ship going to the readers' shores in a terrible storm"[2].

During perestroika, many works 'returned' to Russia: classics of the XX century that had been suppressed; works of the period of Thaw, which had exceeded the limits of the framework set by Thaw; émigré literature; and avant-garde and modernist literature of the '70s and '80s. Many of these works had been published in the *tamizdat*—that is, abroad, or in the *samizdat*—that is, published by 'oneself', underground. To this list one must add self-censored literature, like *The White Cloud of Genghis Khan*. This was a curious case, for this was a portion of the novel that the author had held back, 'excess weight' that could be taken out without harm to the structure of the

1. All translations into English from texts whose titles in the 'Footnotes' are given in Russian are mine – RD.
2. Foreword, *Beloe Oblako Chingizkhana*, Chingiz Aitmatov, http://vgershov.lib.ru/ARCHIVES/A/AYTMATOV_Chingiz/Aytmatov_Ch..htm, p. 1 (page nos. according to print in landscape format).

larger whole of which it was part. It could stand as an autonomous unit, creating a new genre, 'the novella towards a novel'.

This work contains within it all the characteristics of Aitmatov's authorial style, comprising in the main, the compression of different time frames—the contemporary and the legendary—into one tight structure. Set in 1953, it deals with school teacher Abutalip Kutybaev's arrest after he has returned from the front. The story is set during the time of internal Stalinist purges against 'bourgeois/feudal nationalists' that continued even after the war had been won by the people of Soviet Union. The terrible form of the mind-set of the era, the hounding of innocent people and the dynamics of hate, are portrayed through the character of Tansykbaev. This 'production' of hatred towards imaginary class enemies all around, particularly when the nation had collectively fought and won the war against fascism, only helped careerists in the party machinery, for whom power was god: "To keep heat on the war, more and more new objects (of hate) were needed, new trends in 'exposures'; many in this regard had already been exhausted... even unto the deportation and exile of entire peoples to Siberia and Central Asia, to certain death"[3]. So a new enemy had been found—the bourgeois-nationalist. The unmasking of these 'enemies of the people', pushing them into a no-win situation, and the terror unleashed, caused people to become over careful and to "loudly and visibly negate all national values, even to the extent of refusing to speak in one's native tongue"[4]. One of the 'crimes' that Abutalip is accused of—apart from that of having been a traitor during the war—was that of having written down a legend about Genghis Khan: the Sarozek Execution. This legend, according to Aitmatov is part of "the oral, nomadic legacy about Genghis Khan, a myth, corresponding but little to historical reality, but stating a lot about people's memory..."[5].

---

3. *Beloe Oblako Chingizkhana*, Chingiz Aitmatov, http://vgershov.lib.ru/ARCHIVES/A/AYTMATOV_Chingiz/Aytmatov_Ch..htm, p. 7.
4. Ibid., p.7.
5. Foreword, *Beloe Oblako Chingizkhana*, Chingiz Aitmatov, http://vgershov.lib.ru/ARCHIVES/A/AYTMATOV_Chingiz/Aytmatov_Ch..htm, p. 1.

Breaking the Laws of Nature

The legend of the Sarozek Execution deals with Genghis Khan's conquests westwards of Mongolia, to realize his dreams of conquering Europe. The movement of his troops had been planned in minute detail. Genghis had by now begun to believe that he was divinely ordained to rule the world. He had been told by a wandering soothsayer that a white cloud, a sign of the Great Sky, would appear and constantly hover above his head. "But you must treasure this cloud, for if you lose it, you will lose your mighty power", the fortune teller had said. En route to Europe, the white cloud had appeared over Genghis Khan's head and travelled with him across the steppe. "Even the laws of nature were rejected by Genghis Khan, blaspheming against life itself and God. He wanted to put God at his service..."[6].

Women moved with the troops. There were, however, strict orders that these women must not bear children for that would affect the commitment of the soldier to the Khan's cause. The punishment for pregnancy was execution. Even so, Dogulang, a seamstress in the troops, whose job was to sew dragons on Genghis Khan's flags, not only hid her pregnancy, but managed to give birth to a son. Her husband, Erdene, a lieutenant, makes an impossible plan to flee. Dogulang says, "How will you get away from the Khan, there is no such place on earth! .... It is easier to get away from God, than from the Khan"[7]. And yet, for the sake of their newly-born son, they plan to flee. The Khan finds out and orders the wife to be publicly executed. Although Dogulang does not divulge the name of her beloved, Erdene cannot hide and watch her fate. He reveals himself and both are executed. Their faithful, old Chinese slave-servant Altun, takes their child and wanders in the wide, uninhabited steppes, not knowing how she would feed the child. When she has reached the nadir of desperation, she puts the child to her dry breasts. She is wonderstruck that there is milk. A small white cloud begins to hover over the head of the child.

Genghis Khan realises that the power of the Great Sky has been withdrawn from him when he sees that the white cloud has disappeared

---

6. *Beloe Oblako Chingizkhana*, Chingiz Aitmatov, http://vgershov.lib.ru/ARCHIVES/A/AYTMATOV_Chingiz/Aytmatov_Ch..htm, p. 14.
7. Ibid., p.24.

from above his head. He returns to Mongolia, "... to be buried god knows where"[8], leaving the conquest of the West to his sons and grandsons.

The Lust for Power

Aitmatov's depiction of Genghis Khan's lust for power has echoes of Raskolnikov's "all is permitted" in Dostoevsky's *Crime and Punishment*. The difference however, is that this dictum is no longer of the individual who is debating with his conscience, but of the State that has no qualms of conscience. Aitmatov in this work, shows how Genghis Khan develops from an individual clansman who has to defend himself, his family and clan into the all-powerful head of nomadic governance. The corruption occurs step-by-step. He is afraid that the God above in the Great Sky will punish him, but grows more daring, when no retribution visits him: "But the Sky did not show any anger, in no way did it manifest its displeasure, and did not withdraw its unlimited grace. And as in a game of chance, everything was played as a gamble, and risk, as a challenge to that which was considered the justice of the Sky, and experienced as the tolerance of the Sky. Each time, the Sky withstood the challenge! And from this he came to the conclusion that all was permitted to him. And with the passing years the conviction that he was the Chosen One of the Sky, the son of the Sky, grew stronger"[9]. There is a hint of criticism also of those who could have stopped these excursions outside the limits of justice, whose 'tolerance' contributes to the manic obsession with power. The more power he had, the more he wanted, and the more he considered himself to be superhuman. "In this paranoid idea, this increasing greed of being an absolute power, lay the cruel essence of the emperor of the steppes and his historical role"[10].

Genghis Khan prepared for the advance on Europe for two years "... taking account of even the smallest detail. From trustworthy agents and spies, merchants and pilgrims, from travelling dervishes, from Chinese tradesmen, Uighurs, Arabs and Persians, he collected information so that he knew all that was needed to be known about

8. Ibid., p. 41.
9. Ibid., pp. 17-18.
10. Ibid., p. 13.

the best routes and passes for the movement of his vast troops"[11]. This information gathering system, in which he had managed to recruit people of all nations, contributed to the establishing of his great empire, and it once again has resonances in contemporary Soviet reality. Yet, ironically, this well-oiled spy system failed to bring him, for over nine months, the news of Dogulang's expected child.

Aitmatov also draws attention to the way in which one man's manic wishes are realized by the mass of people whom he controls and holds in fear, but also, paradoxically infuses and binds with his ideas. "The Khan's mania and will was achieved with great preparedness; and tens of thousands of people willingly went along, exploited and inspired by him, lusting for more fame, power and land"[12]. This is the new turn in Aitmatov work in the '90s; he is increasingly engaged with the mass scale of violence, a theme taken up with great force once again in *The Mark of Cassandra*.

Hope for the Future

According to Tansykbaev, " 'The Legend of the Mankurts'—was a harmful call to the resurrection of the unnecessary and forgotten language of one's ancestors, against the assimilation of nations, and the 'Sarozek Execution' was a judgement on the powerful supreme power, an undermining of the priority that interests of the state had over that of the individual; it expressed a sympathy for decadent bourgeois individualism, a rejection of the general line of collectivization... and from here the negation of socialism was not far"[13]. But this legend is resurrected in the minds of people, because it shows that rebellion can occur even in states which control its citizens absolutely. It is conscience that pushes those who are fragile to rebellion, even though they know the consequence may be death.

The breaking of social orders and the intermingling of peoples and the relations of power are also envisaged in the image of the child born in love and rebellion, who will be brought up by a lowly servant and protected by divinity. The school teacher Abutalip commits suicide, knowing he can never prove his innocence to that

11. Ibid., pp.13-14.
12. Ibid., p. 16.
13. Ibid., p. 43.

representative of the Devil, Tansykbaev, or to the State. Yet in the long and moving passage describing Abutalip's deportation, he sees his home by the train tracks, his beloved wife, children and friends through the windows of his train compartment. Aitmatov creates an image of them in which they seem to be in a time-bubble. This 'time bubble image' and the evocation of a legend from people's memory, carry within themselves the seeds of optimism, that some things do endure, despite Abutalip's tragic end. The image of the train itself is an important one in this novella because there are autobiographical references in it. In an interview Aitmatov has said: "The railroad brought us everything, so to say. On that railroad my father left to study in Moscow. On the same line he returned in a prison wagon for his investigation. The same railroad was used to take him away to the north somewhere, perhaps to Chukotka, or maybe he disappeared somewhere else. Who knows? .... It was as if Father and Grandfather built that tunnel for our fate"[14].

Cultural signs can be Janus-faced. This is particularly true when they are used by the powerless to subvert given meanings. Dogulang is a seamstress, who according to Altun, has magic in her hands: "The dragons she embroiders run on the banners, as if they are alive. The stars glow on the sheet as if they are in the sky. I am telling you, she is a master-craftsman blessed by god"[15]. She embroiders dragons, Genghis Khan's logo, on banners. But the dragon for this seamstress, stands not for the Khan, but her beloved. "I embroider dragons on the banners. No one knows, they are all—you.... It is you, your embodiment in the dragon, that I stitch on the banners"[16]. Just as the dragon can be interpreted in two ways, the Sarozek Execution legend, inserted into the narrative of the post-war Stalinist times lends itself to many interpretations.

---

14. *The Parables from the Past: The Prose Fiction of Chingiz Aitmatov*, Joseph P. Mozur, University of Pittsburgh Press, 1995, p. 20.
15. *Beloe Oblako Chingizkhana*, Chingiz Aitmatov, http://vgershov.lib.ru/ARCHIVES/A/AYTMATOV_Chingiz/Aytmatov_Ch..htm, p.27.
16. Ibid., p. 23.

III

ETHICS IN THE TIME OF DYSTOPIA
The Mark of Cassandra

And thus expands the Universe, through pain and suffering.
—'The Mark Of Cassandra'[1]

Aitmatov's 1994 novel[2], *The Mark of Cassandra*, marks a break from his earlier work. The earlier rootedness of the text in a Kyrgyz frame of reference is absent, even though themes familiar to his work such as power, repression and corruption juxtaposed with the idealism and fragile beauty of the fighting human spirit are being elaborated. In *The Mark of Cassandra*, the framework of reference is global and Kyrgyzstan is absent. This has invited criticism, for Aitmatov was not just any writer, but a cultural icon, who had found a way of articulating a critique of socialism in the Soviet Union and also of debating with the canons of socialist realism in his works. Aitmatov's works, through the decades were greeted not merely as literary events, but as a *cultural* events in the life of the people. He was also a writer who was feted by the State, receiving innumerable awards, and one of the artists who practiced 'socialist realism with a human face'. He represented, in a sense, despite his critical positions (which were often self-censored or censored by state organs), the triumph of socialism in the Asian republics. That such a

1. *Tavro Kassandry*, Chingiz Aitmatov, Moscow, Zhusupbalasagin, 1995, p. 129. All further references to the novel are from this edition.
2. The novel was first published in 1994 in the journal *Znamya*.

talent could flower, amalgamating local narrative traditions with the concerns of socialist realism in a constructively polemical way, and confront the broader issues of the time, was a sign of the positive dialectic between Russia and the Central Asian republics. *The Mark of Cassandra* has, therefore, invited criticism, not the least for Aitmatov's having conveniently gone global after the collapse of the Soviet Union[3]. Aktan Abdykalykov, the well-known Kyrgyz filmmaker, says of his even better-known compatriot: "He was my favourite writer and he certainly influenced me. But I liked the earlier Aitmatov. I don't like the wise old Aitmatov. I think his thinking has become more European and I think he is wrong.... *Jamilia* was a wonderful novel. I think Kyrgyz people need that kind of understanding of Kyrgyz mentality. His themes have become very global. Do we need books like *The Mark of Cassandra*? I think of Aitmatov this way because I want to remind myself not to step over this barrier. Don't shoot films about general global issues from somewhere in Paris! Aitmatov would not be mad at me for saying this, he would agree with me"[4]. Abdykalykov's criticism is representative of the irritation many Aitmatov followers have felt over the novel. Aitmatov, too, has noted that the response to the novel was not the one he had expected:

> "It is true that I am finding a response mainly from European readers—German, Italian and French.
>
> I hoped that Russian literary criticism would support my novel, or at least draw the attention of the reader to it. But this did not happen"[5].

---

3. See for instance, '*Chingiz Aitmatov kak zerkalo russkoi mechty*' in *Russkij Zhurnal*, Vladimir Tuchkov, 21.4.1999 : "The view on the world as a unitary organism, which is quite seriously sick, has for some time been appearing in Aitmatov's prose in apocalyptic images. And now, as a successful ambassador in a comfortable country, Chingiz Torekulovich has written a new novel, 'The Mark of Cassandra'.... ...'The Mark of Cassandra' has met with skepticism in critical writings in his own land but has been a hit with German readers."
4. *Secrets in the Looking Glass*, Aktan Abdykalykov interviewed by Gönül Dönmez-Colin, Cinemaya – The Asian Film Quarterly, No. 58, 2003.
5. *Chingiz Aitmatov: Stat'i, Vystupleniya, Esse, Dialogi*, Sobraniye Sochinenij v 7 tomakh, Tom 7, Moskva, 1998, p. 535.

The Mark of Cassandra in going global, in fact, continues Aitmatov's preoccupation with many of the themes articulated in his previous works, albeit in a changed socio-political context. The decisive shift from the local to the global, which marks the break from his earlier work, only gives him a wider canvas to expound his favourite theme of Evil and its many manifestations in post-Cold War, post-industrial mass society. *The Mark of Cassandra* is a work of despondence—and not of indulgence—and is probably Aitmatov's most didactic novel. Set in the end of the XX century, after the fall of Soviet Union and the end of the Cold War, *The Mark of Cassandra* is imbued with an apocalyptic vision and gives a rousing call to wage war with the many faces of Evil, or be doomed forever.

Galaxy With a View

The second epigraph to the novel deals specifically with the theme of Evil in the novel: The more blessed are those who have not come into existence, who have not yet seen the evil that is done under the sun. This epigraph sets the main themes of the novel: the themes of the desire not to take birth and of the expanse of the universe that exists under the sun. *The Mark of Cassandra* does not merely posit a 'global' vision; it does much more, it posits a *galactic view* on the state of affairs on earth. This in itself is a radical gesture: the global vision, after all, has to do with the reach of multinational capital; the galactic view in lying beyond the frontiers of the planet, miniaturises and relativises the global vision. As Bork says to Unger: Evil kills our resources to belong to the universe and docs not allow our minds to lift its head to cognize different forms of culture, so that man could be other than he is now[6].

It is from this broader perspective that the political upheavals that marked the XX century in the histories of nations and individuals are referred to. According to Filofei, Stalin-Hitler or Hitler-Stalin cost the earth so many victims, that their number could not be fully ascertained even after the passing of so many decades. The horrors of the war between Armenia and Azerbaijan are evoked, in which corpses were sold back to relatives and provided roaring business. Afghanistan is remembered, as are Sakharov and Salman Rushdie. "In the expanses

6. *Tavro Kassandry*, p. 75.

of the universe, the century that is given to man, is equivalent just to the time given to a fly", writes Filofei in his final letter to the Earth. "Man, however, was gifted with thought, and this extends his life. But this can also result in the opposite: it can sharply cut it short"[7].

The thought that can extend the span of existence in a metaphorical way is ethical thought. Diabolical thought is destructive. "And the winds of human evil are not extinguished. ... That is how it is already organised in our life: doers of good are always in deficit, evil is always in surplus, always beyond limits"[8]. It is conscience that makes the ethical human being. But its voice is often stifled. What makes a heroine of Runa, is that she is willing to stake her life for what she believes to be true, and speaks according to the dictates of her conscience. It is she who kindles in Filofei, the cold scientist, devoted solely to his research, the realisation that science too, should be guided by ethics. In his final Confession he wonders: "Where does the boundary between scientific experiments and crime lie, who can point to that unstable horizon?"[9] On the other end of the spectrum is the conscience-less presidential candidate, Oliver Ordok, aspirant to the highest seat of power in the United States of America. A populist, he thinks nothing of throwing Robert Bork, the futurologist, to the wolves. Airing views that he had picked up from Robert Bork, he realises that these views are not going down well with the mass of people who are gathered in the stadium for his campaign speech. He quickly washes his hands off the position that Filofei is a prophet who is asking human kind to stop and take stock of the evil they are unleashing on the world. He is very nervous about the fact that "The Pope is in the Vatican, Filofei is in the cosmos, and it is I who has to face the crowd"[10]. He calls Bork an advocate of Filofei on earth and is thus responsible for the crowds descending on Bork's house and lynching him to death.

Filofei accepts the ultimate responsibility of Bork's death, for having unleashed the chain of events from space that led to his violent end. He leaves his space ship and steps out into certain death, into 'the space between stars'. When Anthony Unger receives the text of

---

7. *Tavro Kassandry*, p. 166.
8. *Tavro Kassandry*, p. 46.
9. *Tavro Kassandry*, p. 189.
10. *Tavro Kassandry*, p. 55.

Filofei's confession, he wonders where the cosmic monk is now. "Filofei is flying somewhere above the world as a comic mummy, having accomplished a unique kind of suicide beyond the frontiers of the planet"[11].

The Myth of Cassandra

There are many layers of meaning that the Cassandra myth lends itself to in the novel. Filofei calls the mark that appears on the forehead of the pregnant woman, through which the embryo, only a few weeks old tries to tell the mother that it has seen its future and consequently does not wish to live, the mark of Cassandra. Having received the gift of foresight from Apollo, beautiful Cassandra had to bear his curse for rejecting his advances. Although she could prophesise the future, the curse ensured that no one would believe her. Cassandra's fate was tragic. She was raped when Troy was invaded and was later made the war-slave of Agamemnon. She was then killed by Agamemnon's wife. Who then is Cassandra in the novel, and who bears the mark of this gift-curse? Not just the embryo which is named after her, but also Filofei who had made a great discovery but would not be believed; Robert Bork, the futurologist, who saw the true significance of Filofei's discovery, but was not given a fair hearing; the woman prisoner, Runa, who protests at the conditions in the Soviet Union, has her freedom taken away from her and suffers a tragic fate; Jessie, who warns her husband, Robert Bork, not to go out to meet the crowd.... Many are the characters who bear the mark of Cassandra, this gift-curse, this foresight that will only be greeted with disbelief. And the events that greet this prophesy with disbelief are indeed tragic events.

Aitmatov, however, interprets the myth at many levels. The tragedy of Cassandra was that all her foresight did not save her from a terrible fate. The case of the embryo-Cassandra is slightly different because it sees its *own* destiny. The foresight is thus about *its own self* in relation to the world and its non-acceptance of the fate that will greet it on birth.

Filofei is, like the Cassandra-embryo, self-reflexive. While the embryo looks forward at the life that awaits it, Filofei *looks back* and realises that he should not have acquiesced in the receiving of the

---

11. *Tavro Kassandry*, p. 210.

'gift'. "Yes, you should have stopped yourself in time, you should have, as it became clear later, not provided the basis for their belief in your undoubted loyalty", he tells himself. Filofei ruminates on his own condition, and self-critically evaluates his own actions, when people disbelieve and reject his discovery.

Just as Apollo bestowed upon Cassandra a gift with strings attached, the Soviet state gave Filofei all possible support for his research, with an ulterior motive. The Soviet State believed that Filofei's work would create 'the new type of man' the 'future knight of ideology'[12]. Konyukhanov, the ideological head of the Central Committee of the CPSU tells him that the future in this global fight among ideological worlds will belong to "whoever widely opens the doors of society to new people, the X-Species"[13]. The clear advantage of this new species ... is that it will be completely free of all blood, clan, patriarchal and other relationships, which in turn, will get rid of all burden of an outdated ethics''[14]. He adds that "This is the result of the absolute freedom granted to thought... but this is what Plato had in mind—the influence and imprint of the Idea on Matter and the transformation of Matter into socio-political ideal''[15]. Filofei concurs: "But in the very beginning, when the strategic aims of the programme were mentioned, you did not object, did not refuse, and did not try to disassociate yourself. And you were not embarrassed by the fact that you were honoured as the new Darwin and that this programme, never before heard of in civilisation, followed from your theoretical and practical work..."[16].

Cassandra, in the Greek myth, had foreseen that the Trojan horse was not what it had appeared to be, but no one had believed her. The artificial X-Species embryos have been given birth to, by being incubated in the hired wombs of women prisoners who have been sentenced to long-term imprisonment. The women were 'rewarded'

---

12. *Tavro Kassandry*, p.180.
13. The Russian word used is '*iksrody*'. '*Rod*' has the dual meaning of origins, stock; '*rody*' means birth, delivery. The word 'iksrody' draws on both meanings.
14. *Tavro Kassandry,* p. 187.
15. *Tavro Kassandry,* p. 184.
16. *Tavro Kassandry,* p. 181.

with shortened terms in the jail. Like the Trojan Horse which bore the enemy soldiers inside itself, Soviet society, too, according to Filofei, bore within itself children of this X-Species, born before the era of perestroika, when an end was put to this experiment. Towards the end of his Confession Filofei says, "If I could have been on Earth just now and looked into the eyes of those children who were born as a result of experiments in our laboratory!... Why am I writing about this now? Because what we did is irremediable. What will become of these artificially born people? And surely tomorrow they will find out who they are. With what will they pay society back? Will not arise with time in this X-Species an unquenchable desire to take revenge on mankind...? And that I am here in the cosmos and they, the X-Species are growing up there—this is really appalling. I could have told myself that I had never accepted the responsibility for their future, and had only been solving the scientific problems of their birth. But is this any justification?! Where are they to find the guilty, those who conceived these projects...?"[17] The myth of Cassandra is thus embedded in many layers in the novel and serves to sharpen the ethical and moral dilemmas the novel raises.

Believers and Non-Believers

Filofei's letter to the Pope divided people on earth into those who believed he was Satan, or those who believed he was a prophet. What then were the objections to accepting Filofei's theory of the Cassandra-embryos? They range from an instinctive reaction—"What right does he have to interfere in my personal life?" to demanding an answer from him as to why he had singled out women and what he or God had against them. A pregnant woman with the mark of Cassandra poses the problem sharply: "Should I kill the child because it is afraid of life? Does this mean that I, my fate, my life don't suit him? Or am I supposed to construct a paradise for him on earth? And I would have done that gladly. But how am I to correct the world? Or should I just hang myself?"[18] A man, reacting to the stress women are now facing because of this mark, protests that they live in a democratic society where an individual has his rights and cannot be forcibly tied

17. *Tavro Kassandry*, p. 210.
18. *Tavro Kassandry*, p. 87.

to a given way of life based on some laboratory tests. The more aggressive Americans react by stating that they will not put up with a Russian agent disrupting their life from within.

The people who understand the challenge thrown by Filofei's discoveries are clearly outnumbered by those swayed by populist slogans. Bork understands that the flickering out of the wish to live, signals the end of human civilisation. The end of mankind is hidden deep within itself. The cosmic monk's discovery of the Cassandra-embryo has posed a philosophical question for mankind: either we live as we did, or in an attempt to understand the increasing umber of such embryos, change our ways. Unger points to the contemporary crisis of civilisation. In such circumstances the very birth of a child is likened to coming out on a mine field. "And the question arises, even if idealistic and absurd: what if humankind had developed without having developed weapons and not knowing wars? Would man then have been the same being that he is now, would our civilisation have been the same as it is now, or would something quite different have ruled this earth and would humankind have been qualitatively different?"[19] Filofei himself believes that the Cassandra-embryos have resulted from "the uninterrupted sedimentation of evil in us, in our very actions and thoughts, and is now telling on the genetic code of humankind, bringing the crisis closer"[20].

Of Masses and Mobs

Aitmatov places this debate of the believers and non-believers of Filofei's discoveries in the dual framework of mass society and the society of the spectacle. Whether it is Newberry, USA or the Red Square, Russia, masses have turned into mobs in the late XX century. Bork's wife, after the fiasco at the presidential campaign where her husband was called a fanatic who would serve Satan, expresses her fear of the mob: "In my heart after this barbarism, it is as if we are wandering in a forest that has caught fire... and what remains is black, scorched earth, and around us nothing—everything is empty, black and dead"[21]. The grip of populism on the masses is also referred to—

19. *Tavro Kassandry*, p. 124.
20. *Tavro Kassandry*, p. 161.
21. *Tavro Kassandry*, p. 102.

"Everybody loses their senses over one personality and this personality loses his head over everyone"[22]. There is a parallel drawn between Ordok and Goebbels, in the way the former manipulates information.

In Russia, too, the large crowds that served the party and state as disciplined masses have also turned into an unruly affair. The two demonstrations, one in favour of further militarisation and the other for peace is witness to a spectacle where a young girl sets herself on fire in protest. Thus, in the post-Cold War period, according to Aitmatov, whether it is the USA or Russia, rational discourse is marginalised and the law of the mob prevails. Those who stood for Truth, whether it was Robert Bork or Runa or Filofei (though rather late in life), had to pay for it with their lives.

The other aspect of this information society that Aitmatov subjects to severe criticism is the cannibalistic and insensitive nature of media reporting. Everything is made into spectacle. Even the most tragic of events are designed to provide spectavised pleasure. The girl who sets herself on fire, the young fundamentalists who set afire a hotel in a Turkish city in which a meeting to support Salman Rushdie was being held, Filofei's 'public suicide' caught on television—all are spectacles of mass society, contributing in their own way as catalysts in turning crowds and masses into mobs. Filofei in his letter to the Pope refers to a particularly horrible chapter in the Afghan war, in which dead bodies were mined and thrown so that they were visible. Relatives and children approaching the bodies to bury them, were blown up as well. All this was carefully recorded on film. "But who are they," asks Filofei, "following such events on the screen with professional pleasure? And the criminals who constructed such traps of death, carefully fixing their results on film, who are they, and from where have they come?.... From where?.... It seems that the question is rhetorical... but that doesn't make things any easier"[23].

Vision of Utopia

Mass society, greedy for spectacles, by its very nature is antithetical to any concept of utopia. Jessie characterises the attack on Filofei and her husband as the latest in the series of attacks on

22. *Tavro Kassandry*, p. 48.
23. *Tavro Kassandry*, p. 26.

idealism that has happened since time immemorial. "I remembered your beloved Socrates," she tells Bork, "In the same way then, as now, and many ages hereafter, will the crowd stand in opposition to an idealist utopia"[24].

It is Robert Bork in the novel who carries within himself a vision of utopia. It is in the chronotopic[25] construction of Bork's vision that Aitmatov once again draws upon many modes of representation from his Soviet-Kyrgyz phase. It is in this that we are presented with a vision of the world that is galactic rather that political: if the latter deals with the post-Cold War era, the former posits man as ethical being in nature and the universe. If in the presentation of the contemporary scenario of mass society, Aitmatov *lays out* the main actors of the Cold War, the USA and Russia, *side by side, as spatial contrast*, in the visions of utopia Aitmatov offers us a *continuum, an unbroken chain of being* which includes within it, nature, animals, humankind, the galaxy and interestingly enough, even technology in its benign form. The USA sections are described realistically, with an engagement with the chronotope of the everyday (for example, Bork's family and professional life are represented in fairly profuse detail). The first descriptions of Moscow, in contrast, are of city of ghosts at night, deserted and watched over by an owl. It is only in the mass scenes of demonstrations later, or in Filofei's Confession in the end that we see a 'living' Russia. In fact, Russia and the USA appear as obverse mirror-images of one another. Situational rhymes as thematic devices have been used, where events 'identical-in-difference' occur in the different worlds represented in the novel (crowds in the heat of emotion; anarchic, rebellious youth in Moscow—conformist, consumerist son-in-law of Bork in the USA; Filofei wondering why whales were dying the Atlantic just before his own suicide, even though he did not know of Bork's fascination for whales; the image of two suns on the horizon in Filofei's letter to the Pope, two suns on the horizon in Bork's dream....)

In the utopic continuum mode that Robert Bork exemplifies, he

---

24. *Tavro Kassandry*, p. 100.
25. A concept formulated by the Russian thinker, Mikhail Bakhtin, chronotope is the space-time construct in literature that has genric implications.

sees his fate as being linked in a deep way to whales. He often dreamt of them and imagined himself swimming in the waters of the Atlantic with them. "And on that night, sitting in front of the computer, on whose monitor ran the lines of his article, which was to appear in the newspaper on the morrow, he once again heard the anxious breathing of whales in the ocean. Where were they now going again? .... Were people again committing unjust acts? One mountainous wave after the other came forth to meet them, the water was stormy...Soon he too came to be among them. The ocean shimmered in the darkness of the light of the computer screen, holding within itself at that moment both the distant cosmos as well as that which had been conceived in mothers' wombs, in a unitary continuum of eternity..."[26]. In this paragraph Aitmatov creates the realm of the simulacra. What is real, what is virtual here? The screen contains the expanses of the ocean, as it does the distances of the universe and the fertile fluidity of the womb.

Bork's view on religion, too is an inclusive, global one, embracing the different systems of belief in the world... that despite the fact that all religions are one, one's own religion always insists on its priority of its version of truth, which of necessity cuts it off from another religion's version of truth and alienates the believing masses from understanding one another. Maybe, it is possible, says Robert Bork, that man at "the end of the XX century can announce in distinction from past generations—that all religions are mine, and I am the carrier of all religions, I enter all temples of all cults and in all temples I am the long-awaited pilgrim...... I was born a Christian, I was baptized with the cross, I will be buried with readings from the Koran, today I am a an Orthodox believer among the Greek Orthodoxy, yesterday I was a Muslim among Muslims, in Japan I prayed to the Buddha.... I am not alien to anybody in my belief in God, and to me are not alien the prayers of all languages addressed by humans to our Creator.....This assembly of religions would then not weaken the idea of God in any of the existing religions, but on the contrary, give to them the qualities of universalism, openness, dynamism..."[27].

---

26. *Tavro Kassandry*, p. 103.
27. *Tavro Kassandry*, p. 81.

Narrative of Dystopia

The Mark of Cassandra belongs to a specific subgenre in science fiction which can be called philosophical science fiction. This is a less-frequently encountered type of science fiction and is one that has deep roots in the erstwhile socialist states. The most famous practitioner of this genre is the Polish writer Stanislas Lem. The specific concerns of this genre are not to be found in the descriptive pleasures of an evolved technology, or the colonisation of space, but the place of humankind in the vast universe, a moral vision in the face of the unknown and the limits of human knowledge. In 1982, Aitmatov had said "The cosmos is not just a physical concept, but an ethical-philosophical one"[28], placing himself squarely in this particular tradition of science fiction in the socialist states.

Science fiction often deals with alternative, future societies—utopias or dystopias[29]. Aitmatov is, in this novel, drawing upon Soviet traditions of the philosophical SF novel, as, for instance, practiced by the Brothers Strugatsky and dystopic science fiction in the tradition of Evgeny Zamyatin's *We*[30]. In the passages which figure the 'call to conscience', particularly those in the letter format (Filofei's letter to the Pope, his final Confession, Unger's fax to Bork), Aitmatov is clearly influenced by the Russian realist tradition, particularly Dostoevsky. The impassioned voices in *The Mark of Cassandra*, recall to mind the troubled discourses of a Raskolnikov or an Ivan Karamazov.

Aitmatov first used science fiction in *And the Day Lasts Longer Than A Century*. In an interview after the publication of this novel, he said: "Science fiction is a one-time job in my work. I doubt if I'll ever resort to it again. On the other hand, there are some vague ideas floating in my mind. Maybe I will turn to it as a device"[31]. In *The Mark of*

28. *Chingiz Aitmatov: Stat'i, Vystupleniya, Esse, Dialogi*, Sobraniye Sochinenij v 7 tomakh, Tom 7, Moskva, 1998, Tom 7, p. 192.
29. However, utopian works which either directly portray totalitarian states, or ironically represent 'perfect states' end up representing dystopias.
30. Zamyatin's novel *We*, written in the 1920s, predates Huxley's *Brave New World*. George Orwell acknowledged it as having had an influence on his *1984*.
31. 'From Aiil to the Cosmos', Interview with Chingiz Aitmatov by Kalpana Sahni, Journal of Arts and Ideas, Nos. 12-13, Jan-June 1987, p. 10.

Cassandra Aitmatov has used science fiction again to raise questions of ethics that relate to the post-Cold War period in particular, and the 'progress' of civilisation in the XX century in the tracks of Hitlerism, Stalinism and the Cold War. In the novel, the societies being depicted are clearly contemporary; it is only Filofei's embryo-Cassandras that seem to belong to the future, but one that is not distant at all. Aitmatov has used it as a device to discuss philosophical question of humankind's relationship with evil. The novel gives an uneasy feel of science fiction in our midst. Aitmatov has cut the distance of time that the genre invariably has as its premise. As Tarkovsky said while discussing his adaptation of Lem's *Solaris*: "For some reason in all the science-fiction films I have ever seen, the audience is forced into a detailed, close-up examination of what the future will look like. Indeed, often (like Stanley Kubrick) they call their films 'visions of the future'.... If, for instance, we were to film passengers getting into a tram as something never before seen or even heard of, then it would like Kubrick's moon-landing sequence. But if we film a moon-landing the way they film a tram-stop in an ordinary film, then everything will be as we would wish it"[32].

The world represented in the novel is clearly a dystopic one, whether it is the USA or Russia. One of the key images of dystopia in *The Mark of Cassandra* is the destruction of the 'harmony of Being'. This is realised through the images of whales, moving in the oceanic waters as beautifully as a flock of cranes. (It is of significance that Aitmatov uses hybrid images—'whale-crane', 'whale-man' rather than the stylistic device of analogy. Through this he underlines the continuum of Being in the world) Kalpana Sahni traces the changes in Aitmatov's representation of the man-nature relationship over the years: "Chingiz Aitmatov began his literary career in the traditions of Socialist Realism. But a shift is already evident in his short story *Farewell, Gulsary!*, in which the man/nature relationship is no longer one of antagonism but rather one of symbiosis, much along the lines of the Kyrgyz traditional approach. The bond becomes stronger in his next work *The White Steamship*, which signals a new stage in the writer's works. Henceforth, myths, traditional values and the

32. 'Tarkovsky on *Solaris*' in *Tarkovsky: Cinema as Poetry,* Maya Turovskaya, Faber and Faber, London, 1989, p. 59.

contemporary world are all integrated and juxtaposed. Moral, social and ethical values are elevated above present day consumerism, family break ups and the alienation of the individual. The traditional bonds between humans and the environment are contrasted with the senseless and predatory nature of today's industrial society".[33] It is in the treatment of this symbiotic relationship between man and nature in the novel that Aitmatov taps his Kyrgyz roots. In *The Mark of Cassandra*, Bork not only feels he is a 'whale-man' but is also preoccupied with the reason for the mass suicide of whales. It is this preoccupation that predisposes him to understand the full implication of Filofei's Cassandra-embryos. The whales want to die, just as the embryos want to: "... whales... are living radars in open seas. They catch the hidden signals of the cosmos. Maybe it is the whales who first get to know of the imminent eruption of volcanoes and silently howl at the pressure of underground energy.....but most fearsome for them are the signals they catch of humankind's violent actions, our evil-doings, bringing about a disbalance in the state of the world soul, a disbalance that goes unnoticed by us"[34].

Filofei is the only character in the novel who changes over time. (The other characters are static and are presented as recognisable types: Ordok, a populist, Robert Bork an idealist, Unger—an idealistic young man, etc.). Filofei is an abandoned child, born during the Second World War probably of a German father. He grows up, emotionally abnormal and wanting to prove his superiority. He becomes a famous scientist, conducting experiments without a thought for the ethics of science. Aitmatov modeled the character of Filofei on Sakharov: "It seems to me that in my Filofei in a specific way there is a reflection of our epoch. Filofei's fate in a way reminds us of Sakharov's. Sakharov, like Filofei-Kryltsov, also created a terrible weapon. And for the rest of his life he tried to whitewash, to purify himself, to wash away his sin and to warn people"[35]. Filofei's life is, however, in contrast to

33. *Crucifying the Orient: Russian Orientalism and the Colonization of Caucasus and Central Asia*, Kalpana Sahni, White Orchid Press, Bangkok, 1997, p. 293.
34. *Tavro Kassandry*, pp. 45-46.
35. *Chingiz Aitmatov: Stat'i, Vystupleniya, Esse, Dialogi*, Sobraniye Sochinenij v 7 tomakh, Tom 7, Moskva, 1998, Tom 7, p. 528.

Sakharov's who, after creating the hydrogen bomb, gave all up and suffered for protesting. Filofei concurs with the Party's vision of 'utopia'—(the society of X-Species, whose hand will not tremble with emotion when asked to press the nuclear button)—which is actually a dystopia. "Yes, in me spoke the classical conformist, serving the powers-that-be, the kind that the intelligentsia of that time was, in its overwhelming majority, whatever it may now announce about itself post-factum"[36]. He creates artificial humans, but slowly comes to realise that he himself is the first example of the X-Species, having no blood relations with anyone. Even so he chooses to not rebel openly and suffer the consequences, but picks an easier time, during the transition from perestroika to 'exile' himself from Earth. "I am not a hero and do not want to be one,"[37] he says. After the fall of the Soviet Union and the ensuing confusion, the Russians forget about him, his 'rebellion' and his experiments. It is only when he writes to the Pope about the Cassandra-embryos that world attention is focussed once again on him. Orbiting around alone above Earth, he is all but God, sending experimental rays to Earth, watching the globe on his computer channel, 'surfing channels' and viewing whichever part of the globe that takes his fancy. It is only the rejection of his point of view by the world, his own late awakening to moral living and Bork's terrible death for which he was indirectly responsible, that make him realise that he would have to exile himself from even this 'godly' solitude. "It is possible to die, but impossible to get out of oneself, to leave oneself behind"[38] says Filofei in his confessional letter to the earth.

The panoramic view from above has had a long history in the history of representation in the arts. In *Walking the City*, Michel de Certeau says: "The desire to see the city preceded the means of fulfilling the desire. Medieval and Renaissance painting showed the city seen in perspective by the eye that did not exist. They both invented flying over the city and the type of representation that made it possible. The panorama transformed the spectator into celestial eye. It created gods. Since technical processes created an 'omnivisual power', things are different.... The seeing god created by this fiction... must remove

36. *Tavro Kassandry*, p. 188.
37. *Tavro Kassandry*, p. 188.
38. *Tavro Kassandry*, p. 194.

himself from the obscure interlacings of everyday behaviour and make himself a stranger to it".[39] Aitmatov develops a new dimension to the panoramic view from above. Human as alien watching the earth from above, but now seeing not a panoramic view, but an image of himself; destructive individual seeing dystopic world below. Benign Bork sees his beloved whales moving majestically in the ocean as he flies over the Atlantic. The owl sees the city of shadows. This panoramic view, de Certeau points out alienates the godly viewer from the life of the everyday. In Aitmatov's novel, too, there is a disjunction between those who will not raise themselves from their mundane framework and those who can fly. But they are not 'positive' in that they can instead experience the interlacings of their city. They are responsible, because of their narrow vision, finally for the death of those who have the panoramic vision: Bork, Filofei, the owl and the whales.

Levels of Heresy

The novel, *The Mark of Cassandra,* in the edition 'Collection of Works by Chingiz Aitmatov in 7 Volumes' has the subtitle *From the Heresies of the XX Century*. The heretic is one among the orders who refuses to follow one or some of the tenets of the religious or political order he/she belongs to. The heretic by virtue of his membership of the order is thus different from the non-believer, who does not belong to the order, or the dissident who actively opposes all the tenets, and is thus out of the order, having first belonged to it. Heresies do not merely relate to the behaviour of the follower, but also to the conduct of those in power in the order, who interpret their followers' behaviour. A follower may disbelieve, but he may not propagate and wilfully disseminate his disbelief in the tenets. It is wilful propagation that makes him a heretic. In the course of the history of Christianity, heretics have even been burnt on the stakes.

Aitmatov builds up many levels of 'heresy' in the novel. The most obvious heresy is that of questioning Christianity's tenet that believers should multiply, which is the reason, possibly, why Filofei sends his letter about the Cassandra embryos to the Pope in the Vatican. There are other layers as well. Life that has been divinely granted,

39. 'Walking the City' in *The Certeau Reader*, Edited by Graham Ward, Blackwell Publishers, UK, 2000, p. 102.

cannot be cut short by suicide. In *The Mark of Cassandra* it is *embryos*, not even born, who decline birth, because they do not like the look of the world they are about to enter. Filofei is a heretic, because he belongs to the orders, but does not care to believe. He goes along with the State, so that he is granted all possible facilities for his scientific research. He is a heretic to the extent that he believed in his work above all else, and not in the political ideals of his State. He is oblivious to the political implications of his work. His is not even a position of disbelief. In this he is different from Aitmatov's protagonists in other works who are dedicated to their very ordinary work, and who are more sensitive and compassionate than the hardened Filofei. It is his encounter with the dissident and political prisoner, Runa, that defines the strange heretic nature of his own life to him. The 'newly-born' heretic then becomes a rebel, articulating his position actively, engendering new levels of heresy. It is only at the end of his life that he regrets having engineered artificial humans within the order of humans, on this planet. He creates an order of 'new believers', Robert Bork, an American futurologist and Anthony Unger, a young activist. He rejects both the major political systems the XX century threw up, socialism and advanced capitalism, and chooses to reside in the galaxy. Belonging to the order of humans and of this world, he chooses the galaxy to be his burial space.

Discussing *The Mark of Cassandra*, Vladimir Korkin quotes the philosopher G. Pomerants on the value of heresy: " 'Tradition should not be seen only as a mighty power to hold on to, without daring to move. It also carries within itself many possibilities, which can be tapped without the fear of making mistakes, of committing heresies. Heresy is the first, awkward step on a new path, the first simplistic solution; a heresy is important because it poses new questions. Not one dogma has been born without a heresy'. ... From this point of view Aitmatov's entire oeuvre is heretical"[40]. *The Mark of Cassandra* is a turning point work, not only in Aitmatov's life, but in the entire debate on globalisation and the aesthetic practices it engenders. Its merit is in its own heresy with regard to aesthetic traditions that Aitmatov had espoused for decades.

---

40. '*Dogma I Eres*', Vladimir Korkin, http://belousenkolib.narod.ru/Aitmatov/Aitmatov_Korkin.html

The Era of 'Posts-'

In *The Mark of Cassandra*, Aitmatov gives a 'high angle' all encompassing view of societies of spectacle, where masses-have-turned-into-mobs at the end of the XX century. He has for the first time in his works dealt with postindustrial, high-tech urban society. The novel is a brave attempt to figure political homelessness on an international scale. Though he is in the tradition of characters like Meursault in Camus' *Outsider* in his being dead to feelings, he goes beyond most of them in his rejection of earth as a place to live in. It is in this figuring of this new ideological homelessness, that Aitmatov's concerns and the concerns of postcoloniality draw near, while yet remaining distinct. Homi Bhabha refers to the 'unhomely fictions' of social and cultural displacements of postcoloniality, as the new theme of world literature: "Where, once, the transmission of national traditions was the major theme of world literature, perhaps we can now suggest that transnational histories of migrants, colonised, or political refugees—these border and frontier conditions—may be terrains of world literature"[41]. *The Mark of Cassandra* can be categorised as 'unhomely fiction' too, for it charts a transnational narrative. This transnational narrative, however, is of a different order from the one that Bhabha describes. If postcolonial literature represents the histories of the displaced, the migrants, the colonised, this is a work born of an opposite condition. In displacements, migrations and colonisations, the problem is more of identities getting layered, confused, split, subjugated.... If the home is problematised, it is because it is lost to ideological/physical distance, or has suffered physical destruction. The notion of home still remains an *active imaginary*. In Aitmatov's novel, on the other hand, it is the *ideological home* that has suffered a tectonic plate shift and becomes problematic, while the identity of the protagonist remains intact. Filofei does evolve from being 'Devil' to 'God', but that is as a result of his own awakening consciousness; *he* suffers no split, or confusion of identity. Filofei's problem is that he no longer has any concept of 'home' even as an imaginary: he has no binding family connections; he no longer believes

41. 'The Location of Culture', Homi Bhabha in *Literary Theory: An Anthology*, Julie Rivkin and Michael Ryan, Blackwell, Massachusetts, 1999, p. 941.

in his work, and the Soviet Union has collapsed. Filofei can hardly be called 'displaced', or a 'refugee', or a 'migrant', because all such terms posit an imaginary/real home from which the condition is judged. *The Mark of Cassandra* thus provides a new take on the politics of identity and globalisation in fictional representation in the post-Cold War, post-socialist era.

New Departures

Aitmatov in *The Mark of Cassandra* is dealing with a wide spectrum of themes that are relevant to the post-Cold War period. He is, as an artist and writer, working with many of his earlier positions. He is however, also introducing many significant new departures in his own work as well in the literary genres he is drawing upon. In creating a character who is happy to be a conformist for a significant part his life and consciously chooses the non-heroic way to deal with the awakening of his own conscience, Aitmatov is offering a critique of an entire way of social being in the XX century. Moreover, in representing both the players of the Cold War period, the USA and Russia as being equally dystopic, being run by the logic of the mob and the media, Aitmatov is contributing to the genre of dystopic science fiction. This subgenre more often than not draws on *its* imagination of socialist states as totalitarian societies to depict dystopias. Aitmatov's novel also reinterprets the Cassandra myth in many ways, to show the devaluation of word and action at the end of the XX century.

The Mark of Cassandra stands apart, not only in Aitmatov's third phase of writing, but in his entire oeuvre. It is one work that does not deal with Kyrgyzstan. The narrative is global, dealing with two political systems—Russia and the United States of America, one post-socialist, and the other late capitalist. Both systems seem to be not too unalike, in the grip of mass violence and mass spectacles. The dawning of conscience in Andrei Krylstov, who calls himself 'Filofei, the monk of the cosmos', a scientist who believes in science for science's sake, is one of the main themes of the novel. Filofei is the first hero in Aitmatov's work to carry within himself the 'roots of Evil'; he lacks compassion and sensitivity, and is willing to play along with the State in return for freedom to continue his scientific experiments. He is responsible for the creation of artificial human beings on this planet.

His encounter with a political prisoner, Runa, brings about a change in his outlook. Sent to space to conduct experiments, he refuses to come back to Earth. Regretting the life he has led and the harm he has caused, he commits suicide by stepping out of his space-station into the cosmos. This suicide is very different from those of other Aitmatov characters who do so because they realize they cannot handle the Evil that will, in any case, snuff them out. In Filofei we have, after a long time in Aitmatov's work, a lead protagonist who evolves from negativity to being 'positive'. According to Vladimir Korkin, "Andrei Kryltsov knowingly paid with his 'godly' life for the evil he had committed on earth, because he understood that he did not have the right to live any longer. Maybe, killing himself, he killed the Devil within himself"[42].

Aitmatov's *The Mark of Cassandra* also stands apart from his other works of the '90s because it provides a different paradigm of de- and re-territorialisation away from the context of this planet. While the other works relate to Kyrgyzstan in the context of Central Asia and Asia, *The Mark of Cassandra* avoids his homeland and represents instead the world systems of socialism and capitalism in the context of the 'larger time' of the cosmos. As Deleuze and Guattari point out "Movements of deterritorialisation are inseparable from territories that open onto an elsewhere; and the process of reterritorialisation is inseparable from the earth, which restores territories"[43]. It is the view from above, from the cosmos, where Filofei can literally surf the earth as different 'channels', that relativises the two major coldly warring ideological systems of the XX century.

The novel's break with the tenets of socialist realism is very clear because it posits a new concept of world literature, a new 'internationalism', very different from the dictums of 'national in form, socialist in content', or 'brotherhood of nationalities', or 'assimilation through the flowering of nations'[44]. The theme of chaos and the

---

42. '*Dogma I Eres*', Vladimir Korkin, http://belousenkolib.narod.ru/Aitmatov/Aitmatov_Korkin.html
43. *What is Philosophy?* Gilles Deleuze and Felix Guattari, Verso, London, 1999, pp. 85-86.
44. For a discussion of these tenets of socialist realism, see *Crucifying the Orient: Russian Orientalism and the Colonization of Caucasus and Central Asia*, Kalpana Sahni, White Orchid Press, Bangkok, 1997.

relativisation of positions is to be found in *The Mark of Cassandra*. According to the Russian critics, Lipovetsky and Liederman, these themes are characteristic of a movement called postrealism. "Already in the first works of postrealism, there is a *reinstatement of the cosmos*. This is a new *relativised* cosmos, a cosmos that has emerged from chaos. ... This cosmos does not compromise with chaos.... But it, from within itself to a small extent, puts in order this chaos through a dialogical debate, organizing, but not short circuiting, this mastering of the 'terrible world'. This cosmos, which was inaugurated in the first works of postrealism, strengthened the view of human opposition to regimented like-mindedness, as well as to spiritual relativism"[45]. We thus find that Aitmatov in the '90s is not just continuing to work with old forms and preoccupations; he is also grappling with new strategies of representation to image new identities.

After the fall of the Soviet Union, many practicing writers, dissidents included, fell silent, despite the new regime of 'freedom'. It is to Aitmatov's credit that coming from a Central Asian republic, he has eschewed being 'exotic' and 'local'. The drive to globalise has appropriated 'others' by demarcating spaces, where they can put their otherness on view, precisely as the 'exotic' and 'local'. Aitmatov, in *The Mark of Cassandra*, has drawn on Kyrgyz, Russian and other traditions to create a work that shows him to be a citizen of the world.

45. *Sovremennaya Russkaya Literatura*, Vol. 3, N.L. Leiderman and M.N. Lipovetsky, URSS, Moscow, 2001, p. 90.

APPENDIX

A Brief Synopsis of Aitmatov's *The Mark of Cassandra*

Filofei	a Russian scientist
Robert Bork	an American futurologist
Oliver Ordok	a populist US politician standing for Presidential elections
Anthony Unger	Ordok's aide
Runa	a political woman-prisoner
The Pope	a young protester

Filofei, a Russian scientist who had gone into space, refuses to return to earth, threatening to kill himself, if he is forced to. He remains in orbit and continues to conduct experiments on the mysteries of birth. The Soviet Union collapses and in the ensuing confusion, people forget about this 'rebel' scientist.

The novel begins with Filofei sending a letter to the Pope in the Vatican. He says that he has discovered a new phenomenon—the Cassandra embryos. According to him, in the first few weeks of its existence, the human embryo can look into the future that awaits it on earth. If it does not like its destiny, it sends a signal to its mother that it does not want to live. This signal is in the form of a faint blinking dot on the forehead of the mother. If the mother does not respond, the embryo comes to accept its fate and the mark disappears. The embryo also forgets this phase of crystal-gazing that it is granted, prior to its birth. Filofei calls this mark on the forehead of the mother, the mark of Cassandra.

The world is shocked by the discovery. Robert Bork, an American futurologist, is one of the few people who understands the ethical questions that this discovery poses to mankind. He expresses his view to Oliver Ordok, a populist politician who is standing for Presidential elections in the United States of America. When Ordok is faced with a large audience that is hostile to Filofei in a campaign meeting, he back-tracks and tells the audience that Filofei is indeed a charlatan and that there are academicians like Bork who want to serve such Satans.

An angry mob of people descend on Bork's house and lynch him to death. Anthony Unger, Ordok's aide, is the only one who is sympathetic to Bork and tries to establish contact with Filofei.

When all this is happening in the USA, in Moscow there is a demonstration of two factions. One wants further militarisation of the country and the other wants peace. Egged on and provoked by people in the crowd, a young protester sets herself on fire. Many Russians call Filofei a Gorbachev in cosmos.

Unger establishes contact with Filofei in his space station. In a televised communication, Filofei tells Unger that he considers himself responsible for Bork's death. He destroys all traces of his experiments and findings and commits 'public suicide' by stepping out of his station into the cosmos.

When astronauts finally reach the station they find Filofei's Confession on his computer. In this he tells the world that he was an abandoned child, born probably of a German father during the Second World War. He had carved a career out for himself as a brilliant scientist. The Communist Party gave him full support because it was interested in the creation of the X-Species, artificial human beings who would serve the State and would not be bound by the fetters of blood relationships. Filofei does not question the ethics of the services that his experiments are being pressed into. It is Runa, a prisoner, one of the many who have been singled out for hiring out their wombs to give birth to these artificial human beings, who dares to ask him if he does not realise the atrocity of what he is doing. Runa dies. Filofei is filled with remorse, but feels powerless to intervene in a machinery that is already in motion. During perestroika, the incubation of the X-Species is stopped. Filofei is sent into space as a cosmonaut. He refuses to return to the Earth. Here he discovers the Cassandra embryos.

Anthony Unger receives this Confession. He wonders where the abandoned orphan Filofei is now, floating in space as a cosmic mummy.

IV

LOCAL DESTINATIONS

A Night of Remembrances about Socrates...

Written with Mukhtar Shakhanov, *The Night of Remembrances about Socrates...*is a play about a group of young people from Kazakhstan and Kyrgyzstan waiting in the outskirts of the city, to catch their flights to local and global destinations. They discuss their own lives and relationships, their historical past and the prospects of the Presidential elections to be held in the near future. Among them is the director of a theatre that has been shut down, Talas, fondly known as Socrates, and Myndaulet, the 'new' businessman, who hopes to fight the Presidential elections. The play touches upon many themes: The nouveau riche who make vulgar display of their financial power; the intelligentsia that wants to flee from these displays of power; artists who served the State and now have to be at the beck and call of businessmen-sponsors; the spiritual values of the people that are undergoing change in the new political and economic set-up; the ties between the people of Kyrgyzstan and Kazakhstan.

The well-known writer, Shakhanov, like Aitmatov, is a diplomat and political activist. There is strong strain of asserting Kyrgyz and Kazakh identity of interests in the Central Asian region in Aitmatov's political vision from the '80s onwards. This may have to do with the close historic ties that the nomadic people of both countries have shared, and their present cooperation in the region. There are also references in the play to the mass protest of Kazakh youth in Alma-Aty in 1986 against totalitarianism, in which the protagonists help each other out. *A Night of Remembrances* is Aitmatov's most didactic work in which he is arguing for support to the current Presidents of the two countries. Issues of negative and positive local leadership have received attention from Aitmatov in his works right through his career. In the '90s, Aitmatov emphasizes the need for leaders of the State to have moral standing.

The theme of elections is taken up in *The Mark of Cassandra*, in which the cowardice and populism of Oliver Ordok contesting for the President's post in the United States of America, sets off a series of tragic events. In *A Night of Remembrances*, too, this issue of presidential elections is taken up and the ideal candidate for this post is discussed. Socrates tells Myndaulet that he will become a hindrance to the development and enlightenment of his own people, because businessmen have no nation and only work for their own personal interests[1]. "But the most dangerous thing about you," says Socrates, "is the absence in you of the quality of humaneness"[2]. The need for an able statesman who will steer this region in this period of transition is one of the main themes of the play. This is linked to two sub-themes: one, the defense of one's own country against 'outsiders', and two, the remembrance of one's own country, when one has left it. These sub-themes are dealt with, through references to history: Genghis Khan's capture of the city of Otrar and the Huns' rule of China, in which they forget their commitments to their own native land.

The Saga of the Empire

Why is Aitmatov taken up with Genghis Khan in this late phase of his career? While *The White Cloud* has a legend of Genghis Khan stitched into the narrative, in *Night of Remembrances about Socrates*, the defense of the city of Otrar by Kairkhan, its ruler, is taken up. Genghis Khan (1167—1227) remains one of the most intriguing figures of world history, rising from inequity as a tribesman in Mongolia to founding an empire that lasted three generations and stretched from the Mediterranean Sea and Russia in the West to countries that we know as Korea and China today. The history of the steppes has been characterized by large-scale movements, partly due

1. *Noch Vospominanii o Socrate, ili Sud na Shkure Tupolobovo*, Chingiz Aitmatov and Mukhtar Shakhanov, Izdatelstvo Turkestan, Bishkek, 1999, p. 462. All further references to this work are from this edition.
2. Ibid.

to the nomadic lifestyle of the people who have inhabited it. Svat Souchek, however, points out that Genghis Khan's rule was unique: "Whereas other such phenomena—earlier as well as later—resulted from a variety of natural or human stimuli such as climactic vicissitudes or political infighting forcing the losing party to move elsewhere, Genghis Khan and his immediate successors—basically three generations—undertook their gigantic conquests only after careful and comprehensive preparations, by means of an organisation that surpassed any such undertaking, and with a universalistic vision which some historians ascribe to an ideology claiming a mandate from Heaven to rule the world. The genius that three generations of Mongol leaders displayed in all these respects, and the dimensions of the empire they created, is a unique historical phenomenon"[3].

The emir of Khwarazm, Shah Mohammad, having fought the Arabs and the Turks in the West, underestimated the threat of the Mongol Army from the East. When Genghis Khan struck in 1221, the major cities of Khwarazm, Bukhara and Taraz were quickly subjugated. It was only Otrar, under the leadership of its ruler, Kairkhan that held out for six long months, before succumbing to the onslaught. It is this defense of the city that is the object of a long poem within the play *The Night of Remembrances*. Even though the city is completely destroyed, one child is saved, and that one child brings forth an entire people who still retain the memory of the glory of Otrar in the poem. The theme of memory that survives, through the most fragile of beings—the small child—and carries the remembrance of the violence done unto it, is a theme that runs through the works of Aitmatov in the nineties. There is a parallel reference, in the play, to the Huns. The Kyrgyz believe that the Huns were their ancestors and in the play there is an episode where Tanirkut, a Hun, who has taken over land in China, gets so assimilated into that culture that he forgets his loyalties to his own clan. His clansmen finally arrive to punish him for his lapse of memory.

The reference to Asia in the works of the nineties clearly point to Aitmatov's vision to have Kyrgyzstan renew its links with peoples of the East, after more than a century of dominant relations with Russia

---

3. *A History of Inner Asia,* Svat Souchck, Cambridge University Press, Cambridge, 2000, p. 105.

in the West. There is, however, a cautioning note as well, embedded in this call to the renewal of ties, and to Kyrgyzstan examining its own location between Asia and Europe, and its relations to its immediate allies in the region. Genghis Khan in *The White Cloud* is compared to Stalin; in *A Night of Remembrances...* to Stalin and Hitler. All three controlled large empires and had a marked inclination for large-scale mass coercion. While the comparison to Hitler, relates to the fascist desire for a Eurasian empire and destruction of cities and people, the comparison with Stalin rests on the ruthless subjugation of one's own peoples and the paranoia of losing power. There is a further similarity in the way that both the Soviet Union and the Mongol empire, rose to a position of power and might within a short time. There is thus a balancing of vision between the East and West that Aitmatov is proposing in his works. The play continues a theme elaborated in *The Mark of Cassandra*—that good and evil leave their mark on generations to come. Socrates says, "It turns out that good or evil words, sincere and heartfelt wishes and blessings, unjust, false praise, or gossip, are preserved in the surrounding air for three years. As an aura. But this is not all. It has been established that the praise of the people, for example, for Socrates, Confucius, Manas, Al-Farabi, Nizami, Alisher Novoi, Shakespeare, Goethe, on the same plane as the curses addressed to Genghis Khan, Hitler, Stalin and other evil-doers, do not disappear without trace, and leave their mark not only on these very people, but on their children and grandchildren. This means that the good and the bad are imprinted onto our genetic codes"[4].

National Identity

The defining of national identity after Independence involved the redefining of the country's relationship with pre-Soviet and Soviet heritage. Two of the overpowering imaginaries in this regard were the heroic epic, *Manas* and Genghis Khan. Manas was a superhuman warrior, oral literature about whom was cherished by the nomadic peoples of Central Asia. Although the folklore did not belong exclusively to the Kyrgyz, it became associated with them after the Soviet demarcation of republics in Central Asia. Today *Manas* has

4. *Noch Vospominanii o Socrate*, pp. 439-440.

been designated as the 'Kyrgyz spiritual object' and is one of the most important markers of the country's identity, with films, television serials, comics, books and operas being devoted to it, and it being represented on banknotes, cigarettes, cognac among a host of other things. Robert Lowe points out that "In the difficult days that have followed independence, the Kyrgyz have reached back into their nomadic past and embraced Manas as a powerful and just guardian who might help to light the path to a better future. This recourse to a mythical historical leader in search of a modern identity is a fine example of the past being mined and adapted to suit present political purposes. This 'made to measure' hero excludes none by clan, tribe or region and stands astride both shamanistic and Islamist traditions. Unfortunately, however, the myths surrounding Manas ignore non-ethnic Kyrgyz"[5]. Aitmatov, too, has been active in the promotion of *Manas*, particularly in the UNESCO celebrations of thousand years of *Manas* in 1995.

Independence also freed the Central Asian region from looking westwards. Kyrgyzstan had to define its national identity vis-à-vis Asia as well. There is once again a recourse to myth in this passage to looking towards Asia. The figure of Genghis Khan in Aitmatov's works of the nineties as an analogy of totalitarian rule seems to reflect a hazy anxiety. Anatoly Khazanov outlines the many differing evaluations of Genghis Khan: the Russian communists today, following the Eurasianists, claim that Russia was the outcome of Genghis Khan's empire; the president of Tatarstan, too, proclaims that without the Golden Horde there would have been no Great Russia; the Mongols, who under the influence of the Soviet Union had downgraded their national hero, promptly renamed the central square in Ulan Bator after him when communism collapsed; and China has for decades after the break with Soviet Union, related to Genghis Khan as a Chinese statesman rather than a Mongolian barbarian[6].

5. 'Nation Building and Identity in the Kyrgyz Republic', Robert Lowe, in *Central Asia: Aspects of Transition*, Tom Everett-Heath (ed.), Routledge Curzon, London 2003, p. 117.
6. 'Nomads in the History of the Sedentary World', Anatoly M. Khazanov, in *Nomads in the Sedentary World*, Anatoly M. Khazanov and Andre Wink (eds.), Curzon Press, Surrey, 2001, p. 10.

Khazanov insists that "The thesis of the destructive consequences of all nomadic intrusions should be treated with greater caution, especially if one discusses economic processes of long duration. Too often the nomads are made scapegoats of economic decay"[7].

The representation of Genghis Khan in Aitmatov's works, it seems, draws more on a constructed national memory and does not address the complexity of Genghis Khan as a historical figure. National identity markers thus appear to draw on myths and legends of the past which are used to construct analogies with contemporary events in his fictional and non-fictional works of the nineties.

Topical Issues

A Night of Remembrances touches upon a wide spectrum of issues from values of loyalty and love at an individual level, to history and contemporary society, through realism, allegory, poetry and drama. The play is not divided into scenes and acts, but moves through all these forms in a continuum. The play is part-historical, part-allegorical and part-melodramatic in spirit. It is Socrates who defines the contemporary situation best of all, in which the individual seems to have increasingly less control over the context in which he lives: "... each person must defend his epoch; those who cannot do this, must at least defend their surroundings and family; and those who find even this difficult, must at least protect their own word from falsehood and vacuity"[8]. The play ends in this spirit: so carried away are they by their discussions that they are late for their flight. Myndaulet, being the powerful businessman, calls up the airport and gets the flights delayed, so that his friends can make it. His friends, however, refuse this favour and decide to catch a later flight. It is in these daily choices that one's own integrity is tested and affirmed in a changing world.

In the '90s, Aitmatov has worked with many genres—the novella, novel, dialogues, drama—and with many forms—legend, myth, science-fiction, allegory, poetry. In these he has constantly responded to contemporary issues and searched for new forms to express new anxieties. He has been deeply engaged with the location of the post-Soviet identity of the intelligentsia, in a global scenario as well as in

---

7. Ibid., p. 6.
8. *Noch Vospominanii o Socrate,* p. 439.

the local context. In this he holds a unique position among Russian writers, for daring to represent a world in flux. Without giving up the framework of realism, he has moved from a socialist realist aesthetics towards a postrealism, to image new issues and themes.

V

DIALOGUES ON THE PASSING OF A CENTURY
Chingiz Aitmatov's Conversations With Daisaku Ikeda and Mukhtar Shakhanov

The nineties saw Chingiz Aitmatov publish two books of dialogues: one with Daisaku Ikeda[1], the Buddhist thinker, in 1993 and the other, in 1996, with Mukhtar Shakhanov, the Kazakh writer and poet, who has also served as Kazakhstan's Ambassador to Kyrgyzstan. The first is entitled *Ode to the Grandeur of the Spirit* (*Oda Velichiyu Dukha*) and the second, *The Hunter's Lament Over the Precipice: A Confession at the End of the Century* (*Plach Okhotnika Nad Propastiyu: Ispoved' na Iskhode Veka*). The books cover a wide spectrum of themes ranging from personal memories and intimate details of life, to questions of the future of humanity, of culture and memory, of democracy and totalitarianism, of morality and ethics, of dialogue and monologue, of ecology and the future of the planet.

---

1. Daisaku Ikeda (b. 1928) is President of the Soka Gakkai International. Buddhist thinker, author and educator, he took over as the third head of the Soka Gakkai in 1960. In 1975 he became President of the newly formed Soka Gakkai International. His own experiences of the war, and the suffering of the people during the Second World War left a deep impact on his life, and Ikeda is one of the foremost promoters of peace in the world. The SGI is registered as a non-governmental organisation with the UN and has organised exhibitions on war, peace, the environment and relief operations.

Both books begin on a biblical note, with a reference to the Word. In fact, one of the chapters in the dialogue with Ikeda is entitled 'In the Beginning was the Word'. Aitmatov begins this book with the following statement: "There is no word without a home. Every person is home to the word, and master of the word. Even when man addresses God with the secret hope of listening to His voice, he hears himself in his own word"[2].

Chingiz Aitmatov has been a cultural icon of the Soviet Union for decades, writing with ease and flourish in Kyrgyz as well as in Russian. His life, in a strange way, reflects the vicissitudes of Soviet history, its bright as well as its dark side. Stalinist repression, rehabilitation after the Twentieth Party Congress in 1956 when Khrushchev denounced Stalin's cult of personality, and postsocialist politics—all have been signposted as significant phases in Aitmatov's own life, through the life and death of his father, Turekul Aitmatov.

The history of his father, Turekul Aitmatov, a communist and supporter of the Revolution, who was dubbed an 'enemy of the people' and liquidated is narrated in many voices in *The Hunter's Lament*. Aitmatov recounts how in September 1937, two articles were published in *Pravda* on bourgeois nationalism and the political mistakes of the central committee of Kyrgyzstan. Following this his father's name, along with many others from Kyrgyzstan, became part of the 'black list'. Fearing the worst, Turekul sent his wife and four small children back to Kyrgyzstan from Moscow. In December the same year, Turekul was arrested in Moscow and imprisoned in Frunze. Aitmatov recalls the traumatic period of his childhood when his father and uncles were dubbed the 'enemies of the people'. Shakhanov takes up the narration by recounting what he has heard from Chingiz Aitmatov's younger sister, Roza. Their mother brought up the children valiantly, hoping against hope all the while that her husband was alive. Chingiz, who as a seven-year old had dreamt of becoming a driver of a lorry or tractor, shone in his studies and became a writer. In 1957 the mother was called to the NKVD office. The officials handed a note that informed her that her husband had been posthumously rehabilitated.

---

2. *Oda Velichiyu Dukha. Dialogi*. Henceforth referred to as OVD. *Chingiz Aitmatov: Stat'i, Vystupleniya, Esse, Dialogi*, Sobraniye Sochinenij v 7 tomakh, Tom 5, Moskva, 1998, p. 244.

This was how they learnt that their father had been executed nearly twenty years ago, but were still unaware of where he was buried.

Shakhanov continues this recall by recounting the harrowing experiences of nearly twenty two thousand wives of the 'traitors to the motherland', who were spouses of leading party officials and workers, writers and artists at the special concentration camp called ALZHIR (Akmolinsky Camp of Wives of Traitors to the Country). Had Chingiz's mother not found a place in her native land, she too would have been relegated to this camp, Shakhanov goes on to say in his first person narration.

Shakhanov then continues the reportage of Roza's narration of the life of the Aitmatovs. In 1975 she had met the man who had shared the prison cell with their father and was now on his death bed. It is from him that they get information of Turekul's last days before execution. This 'history' comes to a 'close' in 1995, after the fall of Soviet Union, when in one of the mass graves that were reopened, a body with the death warrant for Turekul Aitmatov was found.

Shakhanov ends the narration of this painful chapter of Aitmatov's life with the comment that the awards and recognition that Aitmatov won as a writer was a vindication of the Aitmatovs' position, and a reversal of their position in childhood as 'enemies of the people '.

This tragic history, recounted through the narrations of Aitmatov and Shakhanov in actual dialogue, but calling forth the narrations of the sister and cell-mate, that in turn call forth many other voices—of the mother, of an aunt, of an uncle, of a jail warden...—show that so many people are 'home' to words that mark the same history. Aitmatov does not narrate much, but listens to the narration of experiences that were part of his person. He recalls with warmth the words of an old man in his hometown who told him, when he was a child, never to hang his head in shame for his father was not a traitor to the people. (This episode with the old man is also referred to in the book with Ikeda.) This recounting of a personal history not so much by the 'sufferer' himself, but by another writer, imparts to the narration an objectivity. And its multi-voicedness, with narrations of other dramatis personae woven in, transforms the 'sufferer', that is Chingiz Aitmatov, into the 'listener'. "Who is 'I'?' It is always a third person"[3], says

3. *What is Philosophy?* Gilles Deleuze and Felix Guattari, Verso, London, 1999, p. 65.

Deleuze of the conceptual persona of philosophy. It holds equally true of this curious recounting of Aitmatov's life as third person, *in his own presence*!

Alongside this history, is Aitmatov's own, in which he forges, by and large, a non-conflictual relationship with the Soviet State. Barring a few censorship problems, he is recognised by the State to be the leading literary representative of the Central Asian region and the writer who decisively put images of Kyrgyz life on the map of Russia's literature. The recognition awarded to him by the State as well as the warm reception his books received throughout the country marked him as one of the leading Soviet writers of the periods of Thaw, Stagnation, Perestroika and Postsocialism.

Why does Aitmatov, a prose writer, who evolved from short stories and novellas to novels over a period of two decades, in the nineties, turn to the form of the dialogue even as he continues to publish a story, a play and a novel? The forms of the autobiography and memoirs were choices that he has avoided in favour of dialogues. The story of his father, for instance, could be published in the public domain only in the post-Soviet period. It had found fictional representation in a segment of the story *The White Cloud of Genghis Khan*, which was part of the novel that is considered to be the high point of his oeuvre, *And the Day Lasts Longer than a Century*. Aitmatov had self-censored this story and withheld it from publication. It saw the light of day in 1990, in the last year of perestroika. Memories that are too painful to be recounted in first person find their narrations in dialogic form, as do ruminations on larger histories. The dialogue is also preferred for providing a witness in the form of the interlocutor, and, as a consequence, a ready and immediate objectivity that the autobiography as a genre lacks. The following section examines how Aitmatov's dialogues in the nineties replicate and depart from the long and distinguished history of the form in western thought.

Histories of Dialogues

> *'The hour of departure has arrived, and we go our ways—I to die and you to live. Which is better, God only knows'.*
>
> Socrates to his judges, on being condemned to death.

The dialogue as a genre has a long history. It has links with philosophy, science and literature. If Plato[4], David Hume[5] and Bishop Berkeley[6], used the dialogue as a form to stage debates on ethics, epistemology and ontology, Galileo Galilei used the dialogue to stage a conversation between three fictional characters, Simplicus, Sagredo and Salviati to discuss the Ptolemaic and Copernican systems and laws of nature. In his 'Dialogue on the Two Chief World Systems' and 'Dialogues Concerning Two New Sciences' Galileo uses the form of the dialogue to create an 'objective distance' between the views expressed and himself, allowing him the option of 'plausible deniability'. Defining the difference between the dialogues of Galileo and Plato, Bertrand Russell says, "It is true that Galileo used dialogues to advocate his theories, but that was only in order to overcome prejudice—the positive grounds for his discoveries could not be inserted in a dialogue without great artificiality. Socrates, in Plato's works, always pretends that he is only eliciting knowledge already possessed by the man he is questioning; on this ground, he compares himself to a midwife"[7].

The literary form of the dialogue, according to Mikhail Bakhtin, forms an integral part of the larger corpus of serio-comic genres, at the close of antiquity and the beginning of Hellenism, that were distinctly counterposed to the serious genres, the epic, tragedy, classical rhetoric. The serio-comic genres, according to him were deeply imbued with a carnival sense of the world and had a lively relationship to the present (rather than with a mythical or historical past as in the epic). They relied on experience and were hetero-voiced. The figures spoke in a familiar tone of the present, which was open to many interpretations. These serio-comical genres included the mimes of Sophron, the Socratic dialogue, the literature of the Symposiasts, early memoir literature of Ion of Chios and Critias, bucolic poetry and the menippean satire. The Socratic dialogue as a genre was used not only by Plato, but by Xenophon, Antisthenes, Aeschines, Phaedo, Euclid, Alexamenos, Simias, Glucon and others. According to Bakhtin,

---

4. Plato wrote forty one dialogues which were philosophical treatises.
5. 'Dialogues Concerning Natural Religion', David Hume.
6. 'Three Dialogues Between Hylas and Philonius' and 'The Analyst : A Discourse Addressed to an Infidel Mathematician'.
7. *A History of Western Philosophy*, Bertrand Russell, Unwin Paperbacks Limited, London, 1979, p. 110.

the Socratic dialogue, apart from its deep link with the ritual of the carnival, was marked by the belief in the dialogic nature of truth. Truth is not born in the enunciation of one person, but in the dialogue between people. The Socratic dialogue actively used syncrisis (juxtaposition of different points of view on a theme) and anacrisis (the eliciting or provoking of a word by a word, forcing the expression of an opinion). The people who indulged in these dialogues were ideologists; they were not merely engaging in conversation but in a debate about ideas, to test notions of truth. The Socratic dialogue was often a 'threshold dialogue'. The dialogue was linked to the image of the person, the carrier of the idea. The testing of the idea was also the testing of the person.

The Socratic dialogue went through several stages of evolution. According to Mikhail Bakhtin: "Originally the genre of the Socratic dialogue—already at the literary stage of its development—was almost a memoir genre: it consisted of reminiscences of actual conversations that Socrates had conducted, transcriptions of remembered conversations framed by a brief story. But very soon a freely creative attitude toward the material liberated the genre almost completely from the limitations of history and memoir, and retained in it only the Socratic method of dialogically revealing the truth and the external form of the dialogue written down and framed by a story"[8]. The evolution from the dialogical word to the monological is according to Bakhtin visible in Plato's dialogues itself. "In Plato's dialogues of his first and second periods, the dialogic nature of truth is still recognised in the philosophical worldview itself, although in weakened form. Thus the dialogue of these early periods has not yet been transformed into a simple means for expounding ready-made ideas (for pedagogical purposes) and Socrates has not been transformed into a 'teacher'. But in the final period of Plato's work that has already taken place: the monologism of the content begins to destroy the form of the Socratic dialogue"[9].

The dialogues then became a formal frame, whereas the content became monological. This is the case with many of the

---

8. *Problems of Dostoevsky's Poetics*, Mikhail Bakhtin, Manchester University Press 184, p. 109.
9. Ibid., p. 110.

biblical dialogues[10]. Such dialogues are more in the nature of teachings. The teacher—student 'dialogue' is thus monological in essence though dialogical in form. David Hume in Dialogues Concerning Natural Religion succinctly points out the difficulties in the writing of dialogues: "It has been remarked, my Hermippus, that though the ancient philosophers conveyed most of their instruction in the form of dialogue, this method of composition has been little practised in later ages, and has seldom succeeded in the hands of those who have attempted it. ... To deliver a system in conversation, scarcely appears natural; and while the dialogue-writer desires, by departing from the direct style of composition, to give a freer air to his performance, and avoid the appearance of Author and Reader, he is apt to run into a worst inconvenience, and convey the image of Pedagogue and Pupil. Or, if he carries on the dispute in the natural spirit of good company, by throwing a variety of good topics, and preserving a proper balance among the speakers, he often loses so much time in preparations and transitions, that the reader will scarcely think himself compensated, by all the graces of dialogue, for the order, brevity, and precision, which are sacrificed to them"[11].

Whether as part of the serio-comic genres in literature, or as philosophical exchanges, the dialogue has an internal relationship with Power vis-a-vis the State (as in the case of Socrates), or the Church (as in the case of Galileo, who was convicted of disobedience and of heresy on the publication of his first Dialogues). The serio-comic genres, too, being imbued as they were with the spirit of carnival, subvert power. The literary dialogues also give free reign to the imagination, best evidenced by Lucian of Samosota's Dialogues of the Gods and Dialogues of the Dead from

10. See for instance the Dialogues of Saint Gregory with Peter in which he recounts the life and miracles of saints in Italy.
11. 'Dialogues Concerning Natural Religion', David Hume, http://www.anselm.edu/homepage/dbanach/dnr.htm#AI

the 2nd century AD. The literary dialogues are also heavily imbued with satire[12].

The Change in Address

> *My address is not a house or a street,*
> *My address is the Soviet Union.*
>
> A popular slogan-song of the Soviet times, quoted in the dialogue between Aitmatov and Shakhanov.

Aitmatov's dialogues can be viewed in the context of this long tradition of the dialogue in western thought. These dialogues while continuing many of the traditions of the classical dialogue also differ from them in crucial ways.

The most important difference is that of the relationship of the dialogical word to Authority and Power. These are dialogues that are meant to affirm to the speakers themselves *freedom from censorship and control*. These dialogues are thus not being enunciated to challenge structures of power, but to experience, in a sense, the freedom from power from above. The dialogues, whether with a Buddhist thinker, or with a writer from a neighbouring country have a feel of 'variations' on themes rather than a 'dialogue' of differing opinions. In this they employ syncrisis in the Socratic sense, rather than anacrisis. Discourse no longer needs to provoke, to elicit the hidden word; all is above board, and can be openly expressed. There is no harsh difference of opinion, no conflict of views between the interlocutors, as well as any other possible addressee or source of Power (as in the case of Galileo, for instance, who simultaneously addressed the Church and upholders of the Ptolemaic view of the world in his Dialogues). Much

---

12. Some of the writers who have written dialogues through the ages are: Juan de Valdes 1500-1541 (Spanish religious writer, author of Dialogo de Mercuro y Caran and Dialogo de la Lengua); Torquato Tasso 1544-1595 (Italian poet); Francois Fenelon 1651-1715 (French Roman Catholic poet, theologician and writer); Bernard de Bovier de Fontenelle 1657-1757 (French author of Nouveaux Dialogues des Mortes); Walter Savage Landor, 1775-1864 (British author of Imaginary Conversations); Christoph Martin Wieland 1733-1813 (German poet and writer); Sir Arthur Helps 1813-1875 (British writer) and Henri Leon Emile Lavedan 1859-1940.

of what is said comes from beliefs held for decades under the socialist regime; some of it has been newly formulated. The dialogues are a means of repositioning oneself, of finding a voice to speak in and finding a position to speak from. These are memoirs that are also a confession[13]. They are also a record of the writer's beliefs and a subtle self-defence against critics who accuse Aitmatov of having had the best of both worlds, socialist and postsocialist. Who knows what interpretation may be given of one's actions and one's life?

The anxiety, whose subtle presence can be felt through the dialogues, is that of having lost one's address. As the song-slogan sums up, the address for all the republics that were part of a larger political system, was the Soviet Union. The address for all of them, was not just a house number, or a street, but beyond that, the Soviet Union. The collapse of the Soviet Union deprived its citizens of this larger address. The house number and street remained; ironically, the country disappeared. It is this large loss that the dialogues are actually trying to come to terms with. On the one hand, there is an attempt to define a larger global vision, and on the other, to redefine local linkages. This unanchoring has also necessitated a confirmation of positions from 'fellow travellers'. The anxiety of demooring could not be adequately expressed in memoirs or in an autobiography. We thus have dialogues that have the characteristics of both the autobiography and memoir, but are neither, because they are laden with political and philosophical ruminations. They are threshold dialogues in form, not firmly rooted in this or that realm. At times, they even seem to be soliloquies, dialogues with the inner self that need to be expressed, and staged *between* people. Personal histories are very inextricably woven into larger political histories.

Shakhanov in a poem in the epigraph to the first chapter talks of the four mothers a person has in addition to the one who gave him birth: the native earth (the essence and the beginning of beginnings), the native tongue, native rituals and native history (however bitter, sad, tortuous or difficult it may be). It is as if through these dialogues the speakers are testing themselves as carriers of ideas and testing

13. Aitmatov in his preface to the dialogue with Ikeda says: "... here there is recollection, and analysis, and confession in one stream", OVD, p. 245.

themselves as people. Since the dialogues are not argumentative and no great 'truth' is being born as a result, the dialogues do tend to lose the reader's interest. There is a strange mix of Soviet didacticism and search for new truths. There is narration within narration and one finds in the two books there is a repetition of themes. The dialogue creates a sense of 'objectivity', but Aitmatov insists that they are not free of emotions: "In the course of the discussion there were moments when we were prisoners of emotions. But we decided not to 'comb' into tidiness those thoughts and words which were born in the moment of our communication. We did not hide the happiness or sorrow that we had met on life's road, which were known only to those close to us. And in this lies the difference between free conversation and the written genre"[14].

It is also significant that both the co-discussants are from Asia. Both the books of dialogues by Aitmatov attempt to redefine Central Asia's relations with Asia through the ages. This, he believes, is of great contemporary relevance: "In the global context in the evolution of a universal human culture, I see the dialogue between the East and West getting activated. These are the two foundational origins of world culture. The dialectical unity of the West and East seems to me in this world as the harmony of a universal subject, where the West is the power that seeks God outside—which defines their achievements in the cognition of the external world—and the East is forever going inwards to seek God within the spirit—which explains its unique achievements in the cosmic essence of the human substance. These origins for me form the basis of the highest dialogue of world culture"[15].

Aitmatov and Shakhanov define an Asian Renaissance that predates the European Renaissance: "The West and the East, huge regions of the earth, situated at a significant distance from each other, during the course of several hundreds of years, developed in very different ways. In the XI-XII centuries, the countries of the East were richer, in them culture and economy, science and literature flowered.

---

14. *Plach Okhotnika Nad Propastiyu: Ispoved' na Iskhode Veka*. Henceforth referred to as PONP. Chingiz Aitmatov and Mukhtar Shakhanov, Rayan, Almaty, 1996, p. 3.
15. OVD, p. 305.

The Asian Renaissance and Enlightenment began. And the fact of this flowering of culture and the corresponding growth in power of the eastern nations, did not allow the feudal orders of Western Europe to sleep peacefully. The Eastern countries, rich and mysterious, seemed to them from afar like paradise on earth"[16]. Aitmatov dates this desire to conquer the East on the part of the West to the precolonial period. A reason had to be found to justify these repeated expeditions—and what better one than that of the Christ's grave in Jerusalem, which was under Muslim rule. The eight Crusades, according to Aitmatov, called forth the attacks of Genghis Khan from the East, subordinating more than hundred countries and peoples, with territorial expansion unto the Adriatic Sea. Mukhtar Shakhanov distinguishes Genghis Khan's advance from those of the Arabs and the Christians: "The difference of the Mongols from the Arab invasion was that the Mongols captured land and people, widening their sphere of influence, which was their main aim, but did not pay attention to ideological warfare. They were masters of Russia for three hundred years but they did not touch their religion or their language. The Russian written word and culture, their Christian worldview, remained untouched"[17].

The Dialogue of Cultures

> *...The problem of culture, and in particular, the 'dialogue of cultures', which Mikhail Bakhtin the Russian thinker dreamt of, has emerged today as top priority*[18]
>
> Chingiz Aitmatov

Aitmatov does not merely adopt the dialogue as a formal choice of two of his works. It is also one of the chief themes of both the books, particularly in relation to culture.

Aitmatov emphasizes the importance of dialogue in the individual's personal journey from childhood to old age. Aitmatov points out in his conversation with Ikeda that both Buddha and Christ used the dialogue form to preach: "Dialogue is the examination of the internal space of the world.... Dialogue is evidence of flexibility in thought and in imbibing the world. Lao Tse has said, and not

16. PONP, p. 284.
17. PONP, p. 286.
18. OVD, p. 318.

accidentally, that when a baby is born, he is soft and tender (that is, according to me, ready to engage in a dialogue with the surrounding world), and when an old man dies he is hard and immobile (in other words, the dying man loses the ability to dialogue, in the widest sense of the word)"[19].

There is the need for discussion with a friend with whom bonds are shared, and the need for affirmation of those bonds. In his Postword to *The Hunter's Lament* 'Flights of Identical Souls', Vladimir Korkin also underlines this desire for a meeting between people who have similar spiritual aims: "Maybe, in the drama of human existence, the biggest tragedy is not meeting. And what is even worse is the non-cognition of the necessary co-discussant, close to whom we walk by, not realising that at this moment our whole life could have changed at its very roots"[20]. It is of significance that the 1993 book has the title 'The Overpowering Thirst for a Necessary Co-discussant' and the 1996 book the prologue 'The Overpowering Desire for Discoveries'. This thirst (*zhazhda*), and the repetition of the word, points to the importance of dialogue in this phase of Aitmatov's work.

In social life Aitmatov criticises the monological mode of the socialist state: "... not one of the previous epochs, it turned out, had been so intolerant of the word, as our socialist totalitarianism. My generation lived most of its life in an almost mystical subordination to the hierarchy of the word"[21]. He adds later that he "... grew up in a very monological social environment. Dialogue was alien to the Soviet reality. Direct, entrenched monologue—was specially related to questions of ideology, socio-political debates, proletarian slogans, propagandistic clichés—these were openly and in a non-ambivalent manner cultivated by the powers-that-be for their own interests"[22].

Ikeda quotes T.S. Eliot that at the basis of the most varied cultures has lain religious ecstasy, leading him to question whether culture could be born at all without a religious foundation. Aitmatov in turn quotes Nietzsche: "Culture is the unity of the aesthetic style in all manifestations of life of a given people"[23].

19. OVD, p. 308.
20. PONP, p. 376.
21. OVD, p. 299.
22. OVD, pp. 304-305.
23. OVD, p. 316.

Ikeda points out: "Culture, that preserves the basic values, left to us by our ancestors, is the synthesising origin, strengthening the centre. Consolidating the influence of culture (the hieroglyphs that constitute the Japanese word 'culture', literally mean 'to act with the help of the text') is distinct from the forced consolidation from above with the help of power or weapons.... Culture carries within itself norms, in accordance with which man defines what is good and what is evil. Culture outlines the framework of behaviour, which forms the basis of self-identification".[24]

The concept of *narod*, which carries within it the sense of folk and people that is of a pre-modern communitarianism and the modern community. Ikeda proposes a 'depth model' of culture in place of one in which the new replaces the old: "To the extent that the new culture settles down on the old, on the first glance it may appear that the old culture has been destroyed. However, it continues to live in the deep layers and exert influence on the thoughts and actions of people"[25]. Ikeda is, in fact, echoing Aitmatov's imagery in his fiction of the genetic 'coding' of good and evil that profoundly influences human action, memory and culture.

According to Aitmatov, the basis of culture is the people, their unchanging spiritual and ethical values, worked out in the course of thousands of years of their history[26]. It is in this context that he develops the concept of *bespamyatstvo* / 'without-memoryness'. This loss of memory could be voluntary or forced. *Bespamytstvo* as a phenomenon that was forced upon people was explored as 'mankurtism'[27] in

24. OVD, p. 324.
25. OVD, pp. 322-323.
26. OVD, p. 321.
27. Legend has it that the enemies captured by a tribe were either sold as prisoners into slavery or were kept as 'mankurts'. The tribesmen destroyed the memory of the prisoners by tying their hands and legs and abandoning them in the blazing sun of the steppes for several days. On their shaven heads the prisoners were fitted with tight caps of camel hide that kept getting drier and tighter in the heat of the sun, pressing the skull of the captives, forcing out their memory. If they were found alive at the end of their ordeal, the tribesmen untied and fed them. They were then kept as trouble-free beasts of burden, who only obeyed orders. These mankurts became speech-less and 'free' of memory.

Aitmatov's novel *And the Day Lasts Longer Than a Century*. Shakhanov points out, addressing Aitmatov: "It is well-known that the word 'mankurt' has existed for centuries among the Turkic peoples. And however deeply buried the secret of the recipe of turning people into mankurts was, this cursed word was for many centuries preserved in our repertory of words. You ... were able to give it an original interpretation, were able to raise this theme to the rank of a philosophical problem of universal significance, taking the term mankurtism into the international lexical repertoire"[28]. He goes on to add that mankurtism became an allusion to the fate of the minority nationalities in the Soviet Union, who were forced to forget their pasts. Aitmatov, however, is quick to point out that "The closure in the narrow confines of historical memory—is not the best way for a nation to follow. But the full forgetting of one's past can lead to spiritual mankurtism"[29].

28. PONP, p. 125.
29. PONP, p. 44.

VI

CHANGING CONTEXTS, SHIFTING STANDS

Interviews and Essays of the Nineties

The Collection of Works by Aitmatov, published in 1998, has a whole volume of essays, dialogues and presentations by Aitmatov. These are of interest for they are a testimony to Aitmatov's positions on a very wide range of issues over the years. There is an attempt to negotiate, to adapt and to formulate new positions in keeping with the changing political contexts. Independence, however, did not bring with it a *drastic change* in viewpoints. The change is in the nuance, in the shift in tone, in the elaboration.

There is thus a search for new positions to speak from. Central Asia as a larger entity is one such larger entity that Kyrgyzstan can open out onto, as is Asia. In Aitmatov's writings one senses this anxiety for new positionings. There is not so much a need for new positions as for new *positionings* from which old beliefs can be enunciated. Aitmatov is constantly negotiating and adapting old positions to a new location, a location that itself seems to be like shifting sand. Asked by Larissa Doktorova in 1997, whether the changes in Russia affected his work, Aitmatov replied:

> "Yes. There has been a change of epochs, change of systems, and we writers have found ourselves in a new social and creative situation.
>
> The Soviet Atlantis with all its cultural and spiritual heritage, with all its contradictions and vices sank into the depths of the ocean. And writers also landed in this state of non-being, along with Atlantis. We ourselves

> wanted this and helped it along in many ways. But as it always happens, you expect one thing and another happens"[1].

Nowhere is the shift in the presentation of an old position more apparent than in the references to the repression of Aitmatov's father under the Stalinist regime, before and after Independence. Had my grandfather not gone to work at the building of the railroad, my father would not have gone to Moscow, says Aitmatov in 'Notes on Myself' ('*Zametki o Sebe*') in 1972. This laconic description sums up, in condensed form, the complex process of modernisation and the tragedies it unleashed in homes such as those of Aitmatov's:

> "In 1937 my father, a party worker, and student of the Institute of Red Professions in Moscow was repressed. Our family shifted back to the ail. Then the real school of life began for me with all its complexities.
>
> ......
>
> Our condition was very difficult, but Karagyz-apa (Aitmatov's father's sister) opened our eyes to the fact that whatever the difficulties that overwhelmed a person, he will not fall, if he is surrounded by his people. Not only people from our sheker tribe (this 'feudal remnant' gave us invaluable help then), but also neighbours, even strangers did not leave us to face our misfortunes alone and did not turn away from us. They shared with us everything they could—bread, fluids, potatoes and even warm clothes.
>
> ......
>
> My brother and I suffered a lot on account of all that was being written about our father but she, Karagyz-apa, was ashamed of our feeling disgrace. Somehow, this uneducated woman understood that all this was a lie and that things could not be this way"[2].

In *The Hunter's Lament*... it is Shakhanov who traces the whole history and reconstructs it through narrated recollections of other people. The elaboration is thus not by Aitmatov in the 1996 book, but by another writer.

The Sense of Belonging

It is of interest that Aitmatov uses the word *narod* (people) to mean, on the one hand people from his own republic as well as people

---

1. *Chingiz Aitmatov: Stat'i, Vystupleniya, Esse, Dialogi*, Sobraniye Sochinenij v 7 tomakh, Tom 7, Moskva, 1998, p. 531.
2. Ibid., pp. 20-21.

from the Soviet Union. The connotations of both usages, however, are very different. "If in childhood I had known life in her poetic and bright side, now she stood before me in her grim, bare, sorrowful and heroic form. I saw my people in a different state, in a moment of the highest danger to the motherland, at the moment of the greatest tension of spiritual and physical forces"[3]. The concept of 'people' (*narod*) changes: if in the first quote the 'people' stands for the 'feudal remnant', the tribe and fellow Kirghizians, who stood by the Aitmatov family when the father was repressed by the Soviet State, the second quote testifies to the 'people' signifying the inhabitants of the larger whole, the 'modern' Soviet Union, which was under threat from fascism. While the usage points to an equal emotional weightage, the connotations are almost the opposite of each other in the two articulations. It was the war that created for many a palpable sense of belonging to a larger whole. This whole, as Derrida points out, was a name which did not ensue from a definite place: "... the very name of the USSR is the only name of a state in the world that contains in itself no reference to a locality or a nationality, the only proper name of a state that, in sum, contains no given proper name in the sense of a term: the USSR is the name of an etatic individual, an individual and singular state that has given itself or claimed to give itself its own proper name without reference to any singular place or to any national past. At its foundation, a state has given itself a purely artificial, technical, conceptual, general, conventional, and constitutional name, a common name in sum, a 'communist' name: in short a purely political name. I know no other comparable phenomenon in the world..."[4].

After the fall of the Soviet Union, the Central Asian republics were deterritorialised and reterritorialised: one process could not occur without the other. The concept of 'people', too, once again, takes on different connotations, unhinged from the conceptual sphere of the Soviet Union. The attempt is to now form linkages with Asia. Looking eastwards after nearly a century of looking westwards. Of re-establishing old links in order to belong to a new world order.

---

3. '*Zametki o sebe*', ibid., p. 24.
4. 'Back From Moscow, in the USSR', Jacques Derrida in *Politics, Theory and Contemporary Culture*, Mark Poster (ed.), Columbia University, Press, New York, 1993, pp. 198-199.

Critique of Totalitarianism

In the writings of the '90s Aitmatov is very critical of totalitarianism. In the writings of earlier decades Aitmatov criticised Stalinism, and negative aspects of the socialist system, but it was only in the '90s that he began to characterise the Soviet state as totalitarian and 'monological', intolerant of dialogue. In *The Mark of Cassandra*, in fact, he denounces all dictators as the embodiment of evil. Hitler and Stalin are seen as obverse faces of the same coin: "Any extremism is dangerous. The generations of the '20s and '30s tried to transform themselves into a kind of monastic order of fanatics..."[5].

Aitmatov, unlike Lyotard, does not link the fall of the Soviet Union with the failure of the project of modernity itself. Lyotard links the lack of faith in metanarratives, a characteristic of postmodernism, to be a consequence of the failed project of modernity:

> "We can observe and establish a kind of decline in the confidence which, for two centuries, the West invested in the principle of a general progress in humanity. This idea of a possible, probable or necessary progress is rooted in the belief that developments made in the arts, technology, knowledge and freedoms would benefit humanity as a whole.
>
> ......
>
> After two centuries we have become more alert to signs which would indicate an opposing movement. Neither liberalism (economic and political) nor the various marxisms have emerged from these blood-stained centuries without attracting accusations of having perpetrated crimes against humanity. ... Following Theodore Adorno, I have used the name 'Auschwitz' to signify just how impoverished recent Western history seems from the point of view of the 'modern' project of the emancipation of humanity"[6].

The violence of the XX century, the arms race, all figure in Aitmatov's writings of the '90s. However, he does not link it up with a negative evaluation of the project of modernity, for he cannot underplay the positive impulses and influences that he, as a Kyrgyz, got by this

---

5. *Chingiz Aitmatov: Stat'i, Vystupleniya, Esse, Dialogi*, Sobranniye Sochineniya v 7 tomakh, Tom 7, Moskva, 1998, p. 527.
6. 'Note on the Meaning of 'Post-'', Jean-Francois Lyotard in *Postmodern Literary Theory*, Niall Lucy (ed.), Blackwell, Oxford, 2000, pp. 410-411.

linking up with western modernity, concretely through Russia, and by belonging to that greater 'abstraction'—the Soviet Union. Having actually experienced what Adorno and Lyotard have characterised as 'Auschwitz' in the repression of his own father, Aitmatov retains the ability to objectively assess the historical passage through Soviet socialism.

In an interview with A. Fedotov, where he is asked, with reference to his father, how those very people who supported the revolution were repressed, Aitmatov ruminates on the contradictions of the epoch: "This was a special generation. And a special epoch. The wave of revolution dared everything and brought to the heights of power ideas that it was possessed by. This powerful idea, on the one hand, made them into heroes and on the other, into martyrs. In this was their tragedy. The mass consciousness of those years, as if by hypnotically induced enchantments, lived with unbelievable, utopian illusions that were sacral and bloody. A bright future, the rays of communism, world revolution .... That generation became the hostage of this idea. Hostage and victim"[7].

This, however, was not the only position he took. He has never ceased to positively evaluate Russia's contributions to Kyrgyz life. Asked if socialist realism exists today, Aitmatov answered:

> "Socialist realism does not exist in the way it had existed, predefined, and so on, when literature was subordinated to ideological tasks. A complete liberation has occurred. But at the same time other complications have risen. As it is said, everything was flung from one extreme to another. Now the representation of man in the most shameful form is considered normal and beautiful.
>
> Notwithstanding these heavy burdens, I would not want to negate socialist realism completely. This method had its achievements, for example, in the realm of the realistic representation of people's life"[8].

At other times, Aitmatov has pointed out that communism had a great vision, one that was not implemented: "Communism was not purely anti-social or anti-human. It had great ideas. But to proclaim its values

---

7. *Chingiz Aitmatov: Stat'i, Vystupleniya, Esse, Dialogi*, Sobraniye Sochineniya v 7 tomakh, Tom 7, Moskva, 1998, p. 526.
8. Ibid., p. 536.

was one thing, to realise them was another. Unfortunately, its ideas got distorted in its realisation"[9].

Another Post-Modern Condition

If one of the defining characteristics of postmodernism is the absence of a metanarrative, then this was indeed a rude push into the 'postmodernist' condition. The global vision and the metanarrative of socialism could no longer be drawn upon. A lot of Aitmatov's enunciations in the nineties, in fact, reflect the strange paradox of the persistence of his 'metavision' in these fragmented times and contexts. His attempts to create bridges with Kazakhstan, with a like-minded writer like Shakhanov, are attempts at this recovery of a lost 'bridging' metanarrative.

This rude shove into the postmodernist condition without the postmodernist socio-economic context of late capitalism, as defined by Frederic Jameson[10], was an irony of history. The sliding back from a socialist order into a capitalist one occurred without even the concession of smoothly dovetailing into that other 'totalising' narrative, that of globalisation. The economic disjunctures were only too apparent in this transformation from being part of one of the two superpowers in the world to being a small, independent third world country. The paradox of having been a 'closed' system, but part of the superpower, and of now being 'open' and geopolitically unstable had to be articulated. There is in Aitmatov the realisation that he has to speak as a leader, as one who shows the way. Hence his enunciations through the '90s on a wide range of political and other issues that lie beyond the sphere of the cultural.

This was a different post-modernism, where post-Soviet identity had to be defined through premodern ethnic and cultural symbols that linked the peoples of the Central Asian region as well as with the continent of Asia. Aitmatov refers several times in his writings to the Asian Renaissance, and the architects of this cultural flowering: Khayyam, Al-Farabi, Balsaguni. He even states emphatically that the

---

9. 'The Truth on Mount Fuji', Interview with Chingiz Aitmatov by Latika Padgaonkar, The Pioneer, New Delhi, 11 December, 1997.
10. *Postmodernism or, the Cultural Logic of Late Capitalism,* Frederic Jameson, Verso, London, 1991.

traces of the great caravan routes and nomadic routes have remained in the very mentality of the Central Asian peoples. The feeling of movement here has not disappeared, not died, says Aitmatov. He would like to believe that the region will witness a renaissance once again: "Either this region will be washed away by the wave of many conflicts, or it will become the centre of the growth, the future zone of a Euroasian New Hellenism and a humanistic synthesis of cultures. Arnold Toynbee proposed, and not without foundation, that the centre of a future world civilisation will be located in Central Asia, geographically close to the Ferghana Valley"[11].

Lyotard has astutely pointed out that "... the 'post-' of 'postmodern' does not signify a movement of comeback, flashback or feedback, that is, not a movement of repetition but a procedure in 'ana-' : a procedure of analysis, anamnesis, anagogy and anamorphosis which elaborates an 'initial forgetting'"[12]. 'Post' thus does not just mean a 'period after'; it does not point to a 'clear rupture' from a previous formation. The condition of 'post' involves, on the contrary, a deep urgency to recall the past, a past that may be forgotten in details and to redraw optical images that may be now perceived as distorted. The Central Asian region in the post-Soviet period would have to set it sights on its geopolitical location to realise its historical potential. Chapters from Central Asia's past, 'forgotten' or put on the back burner for a while, when the region formed part of the Soviet Union, are now easily recalled: "From antiquity and early Middle Ages, the region witnessed conflicts between the Romans and the people of the steppes, Iranian and Turkish, Arab and Chinese civilisations. From the geopolitical point of view this region has always been a buffer or middling zone, which would prevent direct conflict. And that is why we believe that the Central Asian region is situated at a decisive historical juncture of its geopolitical destiny"[13].

---

11. Report at the Issyk-Kul Forum, Bishkek, 1997, in *Chingiz Aitmatov: Stat'i, Vystupleniya, Esse, Dialogi*, Sobraniye Sochinenij v 7 tomakh, Tom 7, Moskva, 1998, p. 225.
12. Note on the Meaning of 'Post-', Jean-Francois Lyotard in *Postmodern Literary Theory*, Niall Lucy (ed.), Blackwell, Oxford, 2000, p. 412.
13. *Chingiz Aitmatov: Stat'i, Vystupleniya, Esse, Dialogi*, Sobraniye Sochineniya v 7 tomakh, Tom 7, Moskva, 1998, pp. 225-226.

Central Asia would thus be required to play the buffer role between a new configuration of East and West in the post-Cold War era. To corroborate this vision, events from past history, several centuries old are recalled, conflating, almost mystically[14], several time frames—past, present and future.

In 1964 Aitmatov had said: "I want to say here with special pride that with the establishment of Soviet power, Shakespeare's 'caravan' came to us, in Central Asia. From the very first days, as soon as our national theatres were set up, Shakespeare's works resounded from our stages at the theatres in our native languages, and we drank from this spring, so as to quench our centuries' long thirst for the universal legacy of culture"[15]. A different quenching of thirst, that of recalling Asian cultural linkages, seems to be underway now.

Postrealism

This different post-modernism necessitates a new contextualisation of his works of the '90s. Speaking of *The Mark of Cassandra* in 1997 he says: "It seems to me that in this novel I have found a certain way, and I think I will continue in this spirit. Although this is not a reading that will immediately sell like hot cakes, I believe that somewhere in the core of the human spirit it will find a resonance"[16].

While he continued to write after *The Mark of Cassandra*, he has not 'continued in the spirit' of the novel. Both the play, *The Night of Remembrances...* (co-authored with Mukhtar Shakhanov) and the dialogues with him, *The Hunter's Lament...* do not have the preoccupations of the cosmic scale of *The Mark of Cassandra*. These works are more rooted in the Central Asian region and are ruminations on the past as well as the possible futures of this region. While socialist realism, on his own admission, does not exist as a canon anymore, he

---

14. 'Anagogic' is defined in Webster's Ninth New Collegiate Dictionary as the "interpretation of a word, passage or text ... that finds beyond the literal, allegorical, and moral senses, a fourth and ultimate spiritual or mystical sense".
15. *Chingiz Aitmatov: Stat'i, Vystupleniya, Esse, Dialogi*, Sobraniye Sochinenij v 7 tomakh, Tom 7, Moskva, 1998, p. 167.
16. Ibid., p. 535.

is working with a different realism, one that we may define as 'postrealism'.

Aitmatov's postrealism, however, is slightly different from the critical definition of this term. According to Leiderman and Lipovetsky works of the XX century that had been held back from publication contributed to the tradition of critical realism that had not died in the XIX century. These included Bulgakov's and Platonov's stories and novels, Pasternak's *Doctor Zhivago*, Grossman's *Life and Fate*, Varlam Shalamov's *Kolyma Tales* and Viktor Nekrasov's *In the Trenches of Stalingrad.* Furthermore, works written in the '70s and held back, but published in the '80s such as Rybakov's *Children of Arbat* and Dudintsev's *White Dresses* were the inverted mirror reflection of the truth that socialist realism propounded. All these works kept alive the 'homesickness for realism'. "The same phenomenon is observed in the works of writers who were the flag bearers of liberalism in literature: Chingiz Aitmatov (*The Executioner's Block* / 1986, *The Mark of Cassandra* / 1994), Vasily Aksenov (*Moscow Saga*),.... Evgeny Yevtushenko (*Don't Die Before Your Death*, 1995). These works became the culminations of the tradition of 'socialist realism with a human face' which was born in the years of 'Thaw'"[17].

Traditional realism believed that there is meaning in reality; Modernism believed that there is no meaning in reality. These positions were not accepted by many writers. They neither affirmed nor negated reality but asked a different question: 'What is reality?' "Thus is born a new 'paradigm of creativity'. At its base lies a universally understood principle of relativity, a dialogical conception of a constantly changing world and the openness of the author's position in relation to this world. It is this phenomenon that we define as postrealism"[18].

Leiderman and Lipovetsky state that postrealism is close to postmodernism in its dialogue with chaos. The difference is in the fact that postrealism never questions the existence of reality as an objective fact; nor does it ever question the importance of man as the measure of humanity. "As a rule, postrealist works of the 1980s—1990s quite actively use the aesthetic arsenal of postmodernism

---

17. *Sovremennaya Russkaya Literatura*, Vol. 3, N. L. Leiderman and M. N. Lipovetsky, URSS, Moscow, 2001, p. 74.
18. Ibid., p. 97.

(intertextuality, multiple styles, a playful relationship between the author and hero, the openness of texts to interpretations and variants). But the main influence of postmodernism is seen in postrealism's acceptance of postmodernism's creative logic: the striking of an explosive compromise between philosophical or aesthetic contradictions. It is true that if in postmodernism such a metalogical compromise is realised at the level of the author's consciousness, in the conception of the aesthetic world in entirety, then in postrealism an analogical compromise is realised in the tightly localised space and time of the hero, in the plot or in his life..."[19].

The genealogy for postrealism traced by Leiderman and Lipovetsky includes *Flood* by Zamyatin, *Konarmia* by Babel', *Requiem* and *Poem Without a Hero* by Akhmatova, the novels of Vaginov and Platonov, the works of Dobychin, Pasternak and Mandelshtam. In the nineties postrealism became a definitive method of creative thought in the works of Yuri Trifonov and of writers in their 40s such as Makanin, Kireev and Kurchatkin. They dispensed with the 'author's position' in their works, and avoided important social themes in favour of the 'insignificant theme' (*melkotem'ya*), the existential and metaphysical presentation of chaotic and absurd everyday experiences. The second tendency rethinks religious and mythological themes. The works of Freidrich Gorenshtein, Alexander Ivanchenko, Aleksei Slapovsky belong to this tendency. The third tendency of postrealism is the 'new autobiographism' of Sergei Gandlevsky, Andrei Sergeev, Dmitri Galkovsky and Evgeny Fedorov. The characteristic features of these works are a combination of deterministic and non-causal relationships, the combination of social-psychological features with the uncharted spheres of human nature (which could also be a combination of contemporary themes with legends), ambivalent imagery and the structuring of the world as a dialogue or polylogue of cultural voices and languages, contemporary and archaic.

There was, Leiderman and Lipovetsky assert, a tendency in realism, explored by Dostoevsky, of the non-social metaphysical motivations of human behaviour, that could not be fully explained by social contexts. This tendency helped in the development of certain

19. Ibid., p.101.

strains of modernism and is now palpable in postrealist works as well.

Postrealism thus draws on a nostalgia for realism that has links with nineteenth century critical realism, certain strands of modernism and even 'socialist realism with a human face'. It draws on works that were published, censored and repressed, or published in 'freer' times of the Soviet period.

The Route Taken

Although Leiderman and Lipovetsky name a range of writers in the XX century as postrealists (Sergei Davlatov, Lyudmila Petrushevskaya and Iosif Brodsky, for instance), they refrain from mentioning Aitmatov's name definitively as a postrealist. This is possibly because his works do not fit into any of the three categories of postrealism outlined by them, although the 'homesickness for realism' is very great in Aitmatov. Aitmatov's *The White Cloud of Genghis Khan* and *The Mark of Cassandra* are marked by some of the characteristic features of postrealism: ambivalent imagery and the dialogue of distanced cultural voices. In *The White Cloud of Genghis Khan* the distant times of legend and contemporary repression under Stalinist totalitarianism are brought together and in *The Mark of Cassandra* the two important political systems of the XX century—socialism and capitalism—are relativised. A sense of a 'new autobiographism' is also evident in the dialogues with Shakhanov and Ikeda in which he discusses his life and views, in *a dialogical mode*. *A Night of Remembrances...* is a dramatisation of a meeting of friends who recall important moments of their lives, in an everyday manner. Although this does not fit into the 'insignificant theme' (*melkotem'ya*) of postrealism, it nevertheless is an attempt to capture the everyday texture of post-Soviet life. Adding to Leiderman and Lipovetsky's positions, one may assert that a simple return to the traditional critical realism of the XIX century is not possible, for it is now bound to be mediated either through modernist or socialist realist tendencies of the XX century. Modernism could lead to postrealism or to postmodernism; socialist realism could be left behind for a nostalgic critical realism or postrealism. Aitmatov, who is correctly identified by the critics as being 'homesick for realism' arrives at postrealism through the socialist realist route and not through the modernist one. In fact, Aitmatov had avoided the high modernist route even in his 'socialist realism with a human face' days, preferring to tap the resources of oral Kyrgyz literature (as in works such as *Farewell, Gulsary!* or *The White Steamship*) or combining elements of a modern form (science fiction) with local myths (as in *A Day Lasts Longer Than a Century*). His move 'beyond' socialist realism therefore, was a dialogue with the canon of socialist realism as manifested in the change in the 'author's position', the representation of the 'positive hero' and the 'revolutionary optimism' that was to infuse even works critical of this or that aspect of the system.

According to the tenets of realism and socialist realism, a character was defined through his social context. There was the need to represent 'typical characters in typical contexts'. However, the nostalgia for realism in post-Soviet times is a difficult proposition, for how are 'typical' characters to be represented in fluctuating, atypical times? Thus, the very premise of realism, that the 'type' and the 'social context' are perceived as stable givens, is now under question.

The 'author's position' changed, not so much because Aitmatov's views changed but because the context changed. The context not only changed, but turned into its opposite. Part of the larger Union of Soviet Socialist Republics, Kyrgyzstan was now an independent country. Socialism was dismantled. None of the earlier markers of identity, however painful, were now applicable. One was left with the old positions, in a new context. This probably accounts for the near obsessive need for Aitmatov to go on airing his views, and to go on speaking and publishing on issues of a global scale. In a sense, this speech is the obverse side of the silence of other writers, who put away their pens in the post-Soviet period. Both speech and silence, it seems, are two sides of the same coin.

The hero, too, has changed. The 'positive hero' of socialist realism could no longer be embedded in imagery since socialism had itself exited from existence. Larissa Doktorova points out that in *The Mark of Cassandra* the protagonist is not a worker, but an intellectual. Aitmatov responds that "Intellectuals should now accept that the main responsibility of the future lies on them. In our country the hero–worker was characteristic of socialist realism. I cannot say that I was outside the influence of socialist realism with its cult of the ordinary man. I took it all literally and therefore the more strong characters in my works were images of ordinary people. But now everything is more complicated, because I cannot represent the '*chelnochnik*', a man who is insulted and who, in turn, insults. In *The Mark of Cassandra* I tried to rise above everyday life, above politics, above nationality"[20].

The revolutionary optimism of the previous canon, too, could hardly be insisted upon, now that the very social, historical and political basis of that canon had been dismantled. Thus if in previous works, the critique of the system is counter-balanced with an optimistic ending, either voluntarily (as in *Farewell, Gulsary!*) or through censorship (as in *The White Steamship*), *The Mark of Cassandra* is marked by a strong suicidal impulse as a protest against a world in which ethics is absent. Whether it is the whales, or the unborn foetus or the main protagonist, Filofei, all will themselves to death and take the step to self-annihilation voluntarily. This call of death was present in an ambivalent form in *The White Steamship*, in the ending that was changed; in *The Mark of Cassandra*, it is the main theme. Both focus on fragile beings—a child in *The White Steamship* and unborn foetuses in *The Mark of Cassandra*—and their being animated with the desire to die for they cannot accept the imperfection of the world they live in.

If we broadly define postrealism as all those trends of realism that have come into existence after the collapse of the Soviet Union, then we must further acknowledge that this new realism is a hybrid form with three distinct 'pasts': critical realism, modernism *and* socialist realism.

The crisis of representation was not one internal to the canon (the way, for instance, the crisis of realism gave birth to modernism), or a crisis born of migration or exile (where despite the new context, the internal position of the speaker is itself not in crisis). This was a crisis of context, canon and configuration of the self and its views. Aitmatov, in fact, speaks in many voices, all dialogically intersecting each other. Deleuze defines the 'I' of philosophy, the conceptual persona who 'unfolds' his thoughts in treatises: "The conceptual persona is not the philosopher's representative but, rather, the reverse: the philosopher is only the envelope of his principle conceptual persona .... Conceptual

20. *Chingiz Aitmatov: Stat'i, Vystupleniya, Esse, Dialogi*, Sobraniye Sochinenij v 7 tomakh, Tom 7, Moskva, 1998, p. 536.

personae are the philosopher's heteronyms... I am no longer myself but thought's aptitude for finding itself and spreading across a plane that passes through me at several places"[21]. Like the narrator in literature, who maintains a specific kind of distance from the author, the conceptual persona of non-fiction, too, is a semiotically constructed entity. Aitmatov, in his dialogues and interviews, seems to have several positions pass through him, which he articulates. These positions cannot be seen as contradictory in his conception of the world, and consequently of his own persona. They form clusters, not contradictions, and reflect the disjunctive times he has lived through.

---

21. *What is Philosophy?* Gilles Deleuze and Felix Guattari, Verso, London, 1999, p. 64.

VII

IN TRANSIT THROUGH SYSTEMS

"Even dreams are dreamed by me sometimes in Russian, and sometimes in Kirghiz. Preference for one or the other is on the basis of purely external reasons; internally, it not only does not disturb me, but I think, it enriches my palette. To write and, consequently, to think in Russian, for me is like shooting a film in wide format"[1].

Chingiz Aitmatov

The system can be viewed as a set or as a whole. The set is a closed system with the interrelationship of parts. The whole is a system which is open and opens out onto another whole or system[2].

The transition from the system can be an evolutionary one or a sudden rupture. Consequently, transition can be harmonious or chaotic.

Theories of the System and of its Transition

Two of the most important thinkers on cultural systems in the XX century in Russia were Mikhail Bakhtin and Yuri Lotman. Ferdinand de Saussure's theory of language and sign systems influenced the theory of literature and culture in the Soviet Union

1. *Chingiz Aitmatov: Stat'i, Vystupleniya, Esse, Dialogi*, Sobraniye Sochinenij v 7 tomakh, Tom 7, Moskva, 1998, p. 260.
2. "The whole and the 'wholes' must not be confused with *sets*. Sets are closed, and everything which is closed artificially closed. Sets are always sets of parts. But a whole is not closed, it is open; and it has no parts except in a very special sense, since it cannot be divided without changing qualitatively at each stage of the division". *Movement-Image*, Gilles Deleuze, The Athlone Press, 1986, p. 10.

from the early years of the XX century. From the '20s onwards de Saussure's theories influenced the study of cultural systems. While Mikhail Bakhtin's model defines the cultural system as a whole, Lotman's model defines it as a set.

Lotman, foremost representative of the Tartu school, was an important structuralist, who was interested in the typological study of culture. According to Lotman, cultural systems consisted of secondary modeling systems at the base of which was natural language. Language cannot exist without cultural weight and culture cannot exist without language at its centre.

Yuri Lotman defines a cultural system in the following way in 1967 in his article 'Towards the Problem of the Typology of Culture': "The essential condition for the construction of a structural-typological history of culture is the separation of the content of one or the other cultural texts from the structure of their 'language'. In this it is important for the historian of culture, to distinguish in the given entirety of facts, a theoretically reconstructed system (the language of a given system) and the realization of this culture in a mass of unsystemic material (its speech)''[3]. A cultural system can be considered from the point of view of given content information or as a system of social codes, which are linked to core forms of social self cognition, organisations of the collective, and the self-organisation of the individual consciousness.

Apart from the study of codes and 'languages' of culture, a typology of culture should define the universals of human culture and compare their characteristics. Each culture consists of a hierarchy of codes. Not one of these codes can be deciphered on the 'speech'/ 'utterance' level of culture. Yuri Lotman also notes that in times of social crises and change, there is a sharp rise in the semioticity of the cultural sign: there is a strengthening of the signifying power of old forms or else a new form of behaviour comes into play.

Any system of culture, according to Lotman, consists of a centre and a periphery. Close to the centre are those cultural phenomena that manifest structural principles of the system. Close to the periphery are those phenomena whose relationship to the structure is not very

3. '*K Probleme Tipologij Kultury*', Y. M. Lotman, in *Trudy po znakovymsystemam*, TGU, Tartu, 1967, No. 198, p. 31.

clear. The movement of elements from the centre to the periphery and vice versa is one of the main reasons of the dynamic nature of any system.

Lotman also points out that each culture system creates a model of its time of existence. This memory consists of the collective movement of the fund of memory, the constant reorganization of the coding system and the process of forgetting. Although Lotman does not define the reasons for the processes taking place, it is important that he is referring to the dynamic nature of the system.

The problem of the self consciousness of each cultural formation is also looked into. From the sphere of culture, some texts are isolated which have a different organization, but are nonetheless, highly valued. Self consciousness is possible when a cultural formation has the ability to define its own specific model. According to Lotman, models of self consciousness consist of codes for self decipherment and the understanding of cultural texts. In 1974, in his article, 'A Dynamic Model of Semiotic Systems', he states that there is always a tension between systemic and nonsystemic elements which are characterized by irregularity. The pull of one into the orbit of the other gives the model its dynamic nature. The refusal to describe the non-systemic, and to take it out of the bounds of science, cuts at the dynamic reserve of the system. "That stone which the builders of an already formed and stabilized system, throw away because from their point of view it is not necessary or extra, becomes for the subsequent system the cornerstone"[4]. He also posits that the nonsystemic is wrongly stigmatized as an 'incorrect' model: "In the sphere of culture, we constantly come across a tendency to consider an alien language to be non-language, or in times of less polarized positions, to accept one's own language as the correct language and the alien one as incorrect"[5].

In his 1977 article, 'Culture as Collective Intellect' Lotman, working with the method of analogy, states that culture like human intellect is capable of going crazy. It can choose between intelligent and unintelligent behaviour. Any thinking system, be it culture or

---

4. *Dinamicheskaya Model' Semioticheskoi Systemy*, Y. Lotman, Institute of Russian Language, ANSSSR, 1974, p. 7.
5. Ibid., p. 10.

consciousness, should consist of dialogical relationships between two parts or languages.

Mikhail Bakhtin, whose writings on culture predate Lotman's, critiques de Saussure's position on the dichotomy between language and speech. For him, it is the concrete utterance that is of primary importance. The model of culture he builds therefore, is not based on abstract language codes, as it is for Lotman, but on the material sensuousness and social embeddedness of concrete utterances. According to him, the cultural whole consists of centrifugal and centripetal forces. Bakhtin was one of the critics of Saussurian linguistics for its abstract rationalism and its binary oppositions: of the individual to the social, the speaker to the hearer, subject to object. According to him Saussure misses the dialogical moment of the sign and language that is an important part of its concrete-historical existence. He includes the position of 'external-situatedness' and 'otherness' as important evaluative moments of the cultural whole. Every sign, as indeed the cultural whole, is a site for the struggle of tendencies. In times of social crisis the sign reveals its many-accentedness. For Bakhtin in contrast to Lotman, a system can only develop self-consciousness by interaction with the other. In his 'Answer to the Question Posed by the Editorial Board of *Novy Mir*, Bakhtin reiterates that self-consciousness can only grow in the context of an alien consciousness. Interrelationships between one language and another, one culture with another and one nation with another, are necessary for understanding oneself and the other. Bakhtin's theory of communication is a triangular one, which consists of the speaker, the addressee, and importantly, the object being spoken about. That which is spoken about not only interacts with the addressee, but also with the entire network of enunciations about the object of speech. "It is not Adam who speaks', says Bakhtin. Every speaker has internalized language on the axis of 'mine/not mine–alien'. The cultural text is not a non-speaking thing. The thing and consciousness are not fixed boundaries, but limits that exist in and with each other.

These models of the systems of culture, and their dynamics even though they are based on different premises, are of importance in the interpretation of cultural texts.

Debate on National Roots

Chingiz Aitmatov, born in 1928 in Kyrgyzstan, grew up in a republic that was undergoing socialist transformation. He imbibed the dual registers of the mytho-poetic oral Kyrgyz tradition and the Russian traditions of realism. He was an active participant of the socialist cultural transformation of the Republic and was also a witness to the collapse of the Soviet Union and the systemic transition to market economy. Aitmatov is an interesting example of a writer who has adapted to and accommodated himself within systems in transition. His case is also of interest for the way he himself reworks the systemic givens of art movements of the XX century.

Chingiz Aitmatov's works present an interesting paradox of the centre-periphery debate. Coming from the periphery he steadily moved to the centre of Russian literary life with the publication of his first stories and novellas. Soon thereafter he became the star icon of the 'brotherhood of nationalities'. The themes he took up also had a larger resonance in Soviet cultural life—portrayal of life in Kyrgyzstan being transformed through socialism and the traumatic effects of the Second World War, corruption in the party bureaucracy, generational conflict.

The debate on the early works, particularly, *Jamilia* (1958), shows up this tension of the centre and periphery. G. Gachev in an article from *Voprosy Literatury* (1963) 'In the Accelerated Movement of Literature' states:

> "This representation of the Great Patriotic War in the form of the epic *Manas* is not really an artificial stylisation, or local colour. This is an organic and a natural way of explaining the world for the people.
>
> *Manas* for the Kirghiz people—is not merely a creative work....The people who have been nomadic in the past, could not represent themselves in statues, or temples, in written works, or even fertilized land or in irrigation systems. But so that in these conditions the stability of society was maintained,... it was necessary that there be a mediator that could be easily carried, in which each generation could create its own tie with the previous generations. Such a mediator was created in the form of the total oral knowledge: ... legends, rituals, religious beliefs, social rules, that were useful in labour and living, etc. The epic *Manas* is one such universal, self-reflexive consciousness of the people.
>
> The singer of the *akin* was therefore, not only an artist, an entertainer, like the troubadours and minstrels, or clowns and buffoons. *Akin* musicians

> fulfilled in their people not a side but an important function: they were higher than the *khans* and the *bais*. They were the priests, wise men and poets simultaneously"[6].

This review evaluating Aitmatov's work in the context of his Kirghiz culture was met with hostility of varying shades. A. Bogdanov in *Druzhba Narodov* took up issue with Gachev and his explanation of the role of *Manas* in the life of the Kyrgyz people: "Chingiz Aitmatov as a writer matured in our Soviet times. His high level of culture as a writer is based on the high level of culture which has generally become the achievement of all the peoples who were backward and exploited in the former remote areas, in terms of nationalities of Russia. The creative output of Aitmatov has been nurtured on the charitable experience of Russian classical and Soviet literature, which also includes Kirghiz literature, and finally world literature. The reality in which he lives and writes, in which his characters live and act, is a transformed socialist reality. How can one, in all seriousness, speak of some kind of primitive epic thought, even if it is 'transformed'! And can we see the reality, portrayed by Aitmatov, in isolation from the big expanse of our land?"[7]

There was a 'middle of the road' criticism as well, which was, however, was also marked by a patronising attitude to Kyrgyz literature. M. Plisetsky in 'Quests and Achievements of Chingiz Aitmatov' points to the Kyrgyz tradition of realist writing that Aitmatov draws from, a tradition that developed in the main, under the Soviet government:

> "The question of the Kirghiz literary tradition for the work of Chinghiz Aitmatov has already begun to interest critics. Of course, A Saliev was right to think that the successes of the young Kirghiz prose writer was possible through the achievements of Aapa Tokombaev, Tugelbai Sydykbekov, A. Osmonov, and through the confirmation of the principles

---

6. G. Gachev in an article from *Voprosy Literatury* (1963) No. 3, reproduced in *Chingiz Aitmatov: Ocherki, Stat'i I Retsenzii o Tvorchestve Pisatelya*, K. Abdyldabekov (ed.), Kyrgyzstan, Frunze, 1975, p. 89. Henceforth referred to as OSR.
7. A. Bogdanov in *Tseleustremlennym Glazom* in *Druzhba Narodov* (No. 1, 1964) reproduced in OSR, p. 181.

> of socialist realism. ... In the works of these writers there appeared an interest towards the psychology of contemporaries, expressivemess in imagery, a distance from folklore.
>
> Looking for the literary sources of the novellas of Aitmatov, we should emphasize the importance of T. Sydykbekov's 'People of Our Times' more which in its time was a phenomenon that was taken note of in Soviet literature and was awarded the State Prize in 1949"[8].

Symptomatic Readings

An analysis of these critical writings, throws up interesting insights into the nature of cultural systems, large and small, faced with each other in the Soviet period. All Gachev was doing was tracing certain roots of Kyrgyz literature which Aitmatov was drawing upon in his novella *Jamilia*. He was also showing how the artist was wiser and more revered than those with power in social, hierarchical relations. It is thus strange that the article should have invoked such patronizing responses not only towards Gachev, but also towards the history of Kyrgyz culture. If Kyrgyzstan had developed from backwardness, according to these critics, it was only because of the civilisational influence of Russian culture.

The debate, if it can be called that, is about the roots of Kyrgyz literature and not so much about *Jamilia*. Read symptomatically, it becomes clear that the conflict of opinions centers around the placement of a *Kyrgyz* writer within the parameters of a Soviet tradition. Bogdanov, for instance, creates a priority list in the quote above of how the nurturing soil of Russian classical literature, then Kyrgyz, then world literature has influenced Aitmatov! The problem precisely is that such 'influences' cannot be quantified and even less so, placed in a hierarchic order. According to these critics, Gachev was committing blasphemy in invoking Aitmatov's style from the oral tradition of a small republic. It is one of the ironies of history that *Manas,* considered 'non-systemic' in Soviet times, is today acknowledged as one of the chief markers of identity of Kyrgyzstan.

There also lies a deeper anxiety at work: how can certain historical periods be bypassed, an anxiety that is clearly expressed in statements about Kyrgyz literature traversing the path from magical incantations

---

8. OSR, p. 290.

to the polyphonic novel. Firstly, this 'jump' goes against the accepted readings of history. How can the process of literary development that involves many stages including the tedious development of realism as a mode with all its subtypes (critical realism, naturalism etc.) be bypassed in the creation of works of socialist realism? Secondly, how can this jump occur not in the mainstream nationalities, but in the smaller nationalities on the margins? This jump is then only explainable by two interlinked propositions: that the magnitude of this development found in Kyrgyzstan was due to the enlightening processes unleashed by socialism and that Kyrgyz literature had to be placed in the larger context of Russian and world literature.

The contradictions of these positions are only too obvious: on the one hand, the framework is enlarged to include *all* the peoples of the world. There was nothing in Kyrgyz literature that could not be found in other cultures of the world. On the other hand, Aitmatov's mode of writing was derived wholly from the Russian tradition.

That these attitudes were systemic is borne out by the fact that thirty years earlier, at the First Soviet Writers' Congress, in 1934, Gorky had read out a letter from a Tatar that had voiced similar grievances: "That is why so-called approved literary opinion in the great centres continues to regard us as an 'ethnographic exhibit'. Not all publishing houses like to print us. Some of them often make us feel, when taking our manuscripts, that we are 'overhead charges' or a 'compulsory quota' for them, that they are 'deliberately allowing a rebate on the Party's national policy'. These 'noble gestures' quite justly offend our sense of international unity and feeling of human dignity"[9].

By the time of the early sixties when Aitmatov's *Mother's Field* was published, the parameters had changed. This debate was no longer valid, because the writer had clearly moved into the mytho-poetic mode, weaving legends and other local motifs into shared Soviet history. The first calls of the cosmos are also visible in this work in the references to the Milky Way in this novella. It almost seems that

---

9. *Soviet Writers' Congress 1934: The Debate on Socialist Realism and Modernism in the Soviet Union*, Lawrence and Wishart, London, 1977, p. 60.

Aitmatov in the second phase of his work, definitively turns to oral traditions of narration, utilizing that which was non-systemic in terms of the socialist realist paradigm. This was a case of what Lotman called the discarded stone becoming the foundation stone of a new system.

Aitmatov's case also proves that the consequences of opening out of a systemic whole onto another are determined by the power relations between the various systems. "And what happens if we in a deaf manner, close ourselves within ourselves? An art that is pseudonational is born; or in a better scenario it will portray only one side of national character. To barricade oneself from interaction with other cultures, especially if they are more developed—means to deprive oneself from the source of one's own development", says Aitmatov in a dialogue with Michael Kapustin[10]. The small opens out in a more creatively dialogic manner, than does the big system onto a small one. This could be because the mechanism of self-consciousness in the system of culture that Lotman speaks about is far greater in the smaller system, than it is in the bigger system.

Aitmatov learnt his lessons well, as a fastidious student of writing courses on socialist realism. He learnt them in fact, too well and jumped levels to become one of the important writers of Russia and the world in the twentieth century. Almost echoing Bakhtin and the importance of dialogism among languages, cultures and nationalities, Aitmatov says in 1982:

> "In our country, speaking with two tongues is the norm for every person, and an important factor for the development of national cultures. Had we continued to remain on the foundations of our native language only, had we not studied Russian language, had we not adapted it to our needs, we would have been at a dead-end.
>
> I think that many writers will continue to write in two languages: firstly, in the native language, so that it does not die out and remains active and dynamic and secondly, in another language in the given instance, in Russian, so that the work lives a new and larger life. At the same time it should be stressed that artistic works in two languages do not guarantee

---

10. *Chingiz Aitmatov: Stat'i, Vystupleniya, Esse, Dialogi*, Sobraniye Sochinenij v 7 tomakh, Tom 7, Moskva, 1998, p. 260.

that the writer will appear, thanks to this, much better than he is in actuality"[11].

From *Farewell, Gulsary!* (1963) onwards, Aitmatov started using motifs and legends from Kyrgyz oral tradition that became more complex as he moved from novellas into novels. He also moved into a more integrated vision, which drew on premodernist modes of thought in which animals, humans and nature were bonded in ecological harmony. The bonding was often such that it became difficult to say whether it was the animals who took on human aspect or humans who entered the animal kingdom. What is of interest is that Aitmatov, in a gesture of break with 'pure' socialist realism went into the republic's oral tradition. What is of further importance here is that he tapped the secular oral literature.

Realism and Modernism

Socialist realism was defined by the state apparatus as a critical tool-kit to judge works by and a framework to conceive and write works in. Socialist realism in the Soviet Union, from the early '30s onwards became the dominant mode of literary writing and modernism in all its forms was suppressed even though modernist movements[12] had developed deep roots in the cultural life of the Russians. The new system, set up by socialist realism that came into being, thus did not allow the free growth of movements that had already taken birth, many of which were not hostile to the October Revolution. This move to cleanse the system of all non-systemic elements was unfortunate, for Russian modernism was very different from its Western counterpart, shaped by debates on realism, and movements for emancipation from autocracy and serfdom in the XIX century. These modernisms in the arts were often marked by radical stances and an alignment, even if only notionally, with the 'people'[13]. Since the system did not allow

11. '*I Slovo Eto, Vmesto Dushi Moei*', Chingiz Aitmatov in dialogue with G. Atryan, in *Chingiz Aitmatov: Stat'i, Vystupleniya, Esse, Dialogi*, Sobraniye Sochinenij v 7 tomakh, Tom 7, Moskva, 1998, p. 386-387.
12. Symbolism, Futurism, Imagism... to name just a few modernist movements in poetry.
13. Futurism in its Italian and Russian versions varied greatly. The Russian in its rejection of bourgeois values aligned itself with the Revolution. Vladimir Mayakovsky was the foremost poet of this movement.

for negotiation with modernism, modernism went underground or migrated abroad. Socialist realism did not even allow a debate between realism and modernism within the framework of a broadly Marxist aesthetics. Thus the kind of debates that Western Europe witnessed such as those between Georg Lukacs and Bertolt Brecht or Walter Benjamin and Adorno did not take place here[14]. This too, was unfortunate because in the '20s Russia had witnessed very radical and influential debates between several groups that had broadly aligned themselves with the October Revolution. There thus did not exist an official space for a negotiation between realism and modernism in any of its forms, where elements from both could come together. Modernism, in its various formats went into the underground 'samizdat' within the Soviet Union and the 'tamizdat' abroad.

Those who tried to work with modernist elements in a broadly realist framework, had a troubled relationship with the system. Akhmatova and Pasternak, among many others, negotiated this relationship in their own ways. The realist-modernist debate was interpreted in the West, particularly during the period of the Cold War, in the paradigm of the dissident/conformist with a valourisation of the former. This binary opposition did little or no justice to the actual creative practice of artists who were working within systemic frameworks, that may or may not have been perceived as hindrances by the artists themselves. It is of interest that Aitmatov, in an interview, states that he wrote in Russian because his works could aspire to greater heights, which would not have been appreciated by the more narrow aesthetic vision within Kyrgyzstan. By doing this he, in fact, he was opening up new paths of representation not only in the larger system of the Soviet Union, but also setting new parameters in Kyrgyzstan.

> "Various reasons led me to move to Russian. I wrote in a way that was different from the standards and norms of the Party and authorities. In Kyrgyzstan we were more Catholic than the Pope! To avoid open confrontation in my homeland, I felt the need to go to the more open-minded Moscow literary journals and work with someone of the stature and authority of Alexander Tvardovsky. Under him, a few of my works

---

14. For accounts of these see *Aesthetics and Politics: Debates between Bloch, Lukacs, Brecht, Benjamin, Adorno*, Verso, London, 1977.

were published. They would never have been had they been written in Kyrgyz.

In time, I became a Tvardovsky in my own country. .... I am not sorry I shifted to Russian.... I love my language but I also feel that anybody who can express himself in another language should do so"[15].

The Parable in Modernism

It is of interest to examine the different paths that realism developed on in Europe. Realism in its western trajectory developed into modernism and later, into postmodernism. In Russia realism developed into modernism and socialist realism. The latter was valorized at the expense of the former. When systemic transition took place in the '90s from socialist to market economy, socialist realism mutated into postrealism and postmodernism.

An analysis of the function of the parable in modernist and non-modernist writers, reveals interesting differences in their thematic use. I will contrast the use of myths and legends in Aitmatov and in the modernist writers, Mikhail Bulgakov and Franz Kafka. In modernist and contramodernist[16] texts, a narrative carries within it micronarratives, that may be myths, legends, parables, which carry the possibility of metacritiquing the larger narrative of which they are part. In Aitmatov the micronarratives draw on myths and legends that are part of oral literature. In Kafka and Bulgakov the parables are from written literature and not from oral cultural legacies. The parable becomes an allegory in both Bulgakov and Kafka, but in Aitmatov myths and legends are woven into realism as sensuousness.

The modernist aesthetic uses the parable as a an interpretative tool to understand the larger text of which the parable is part. The 'Parable of Law' in Kafka's *The Trial*, for example, serves to provide

15. 'The Truth on Mount Fuji', Interview with Chingiz Aitmatov by Latika Padgaonkar, The Pioneer, New Delhi, 11 December, 1997.
16. 'Contramodernity': A concept introduced by Homi Bhabha to explain the nature of modernity in colonial and postcolonial societies. 'The Location of Culture', Homi Bhabha in *Literary Theory: An Anthology*, Julie Rivkin & Michael Ryan (eds.), Blackwell, Massachusetts, 1999, pp. 937-938.

the key to the many interpretations that can be made of the rest of the text of *The Trial*. Kafka, Austrian, writing in German was working with the modernist problematic of alienation. Aitmatov, Kyrgyz writing in Russian, in contrast, was working with a realist problematic and using the fable or myth to pose a counter world with pre-realist imagery. In so far as it dealt with myths, it had to do with people's memory. Kafka's parable has a didactic function: it shows the possibility of many readings of a text, and further, relativises the readings, by showing each reading or interpretation to be as valid as the next. In Aitmatov's myths, the didactic element is subsumed under the sensuousness of the imagery. It is also a gesture of asserting national identity while participating creatively in a larger systemic framework: "Each of us today is duty-bound to preserve that special identity, those distinctive features, which were created by the people on the strength of its geographical location, linguistic specialities, through the entire history of its formation, since the world is beautiful in its multifacetedness. Or else, everywhere and all over, we would have had a grey, unified, similar manifestation of the human soul"[17].

Modernist movements debated with realism, bringing together often distant time-space frames, or dream and reality into one chronotope, as for instance in surrealism. In Mikhail Bulgakov's *Master and Margarita*, the devil and his goons land up in Moscow. The Devil and the Master recount the tale of Pontius Pilate, a narration that goes on side by side with the Devil's antics in 1920s Moscow. This interwoven parable about Pilate who is ineffective against the Will of Evil in the Defence of the Good, creates a interpretative background for the action that unfolds in the contemporary world. The important distinction thus is that the parable, in modernist texts, has its roots in religion (usually Christianity or in Jewish scriptures), whereas in writers like Aitmatov, it is oral and secular myths and legends, with their broader cultural embeddings that are brought into play. There is another important distinction—that while modernism engaged in the main with the urban landscape, hybrid realisms, like those of Aitmatov's engage with formations in which the world of

---

17. '*I Slovo Eto, Vmesto Dushi Moei*', Chingiz Aitmatov in dialogue with G. Atryan, *Chingiz Aitmatov: Stat'i, Vystupleniya, Esse, Dialogi*, Sobraniye Sochinenij v 7 tomakh, Tom 7, Moskva, p. 379.

nature and humans still seem organically linked, marked very little, if at all, by industrialisation. This has its impact on the imaging of time, for a time that is linked to the cycles of nature has more hope for renewal and regeneration.

Aitmatov in the '90s

The case of Aitmatov, is thus a very significant one for the study of these alternative cultural histories. Here is a writer, who has creatively and constructively adapted to large and overwhelming force-fields thrown up by history. Robert Lowe points out that "Despite the growing clamour from certain republics, the post-Soviet states emerged as a result of the collapse of the centre rather than as a result of challenges from the periphery, and the momentous events of 1991 caught the Soviet peoples unawares. Nowhere was there less warning of the dramatic impending changes than in Kyrgyzstan, where the greater Soviet body had long been accepted. In sharp contrast to republics such as Lithuania, few Kyrgyz had even considered the possibility of independence. The processes and people involved in wrecking the Soviet Union had little to do with Kyrgyzstan, and the small republic could only watch helplessly as the Union crumbled: that which had been violently forced upon the Kyrgyz people was now peacefully lifted from them"[18].

Although Aitmatov's was not an oppositional stance to the socio-political order, he nevertheless evolved his own distinct method of balancing the canons of socialist realism, which was posited as the most advanced, most progressive form of realism on the planet, and a local realism, deeply tied to the narrative modes of his own nation. That is why with the realism of socialist construction in his work, we also pass into the more sensuous realism of the lament, of the refrain, of dialogue with animals and nature. Modernism, well-entrenched in the Soviet cultural sphere in the '20s which later survived in many forms within and without the Soviet Union, left no shadow on Aitmatov's works. Like many Soviet writers, he was critical of shortcomings in the system, but was never a dissident. This position

---

18. 'Nation Building and Identity in the Kyrgyz Republic', Robert Lowe, in *Central Asia: Aspects of Transition*, Tom Everett-Heath (ed.), Routledge Curzon, London, 2003, p. 113.

of the critical insider was adopted by many cultural practitioners, but it was Aitmatov who had worked out the mode of mytho-poetic realism.

In the '90s during the time of systemic transition from socialism to market economy, Aitmatov published fiction and critical writings consistently, at a time when many of the major writers of Russia fell silent. *The Mark of Cassandra* is a landmark novel in Aitmatov's oeuvre because in it he moves away from the aesthetics of the 'homely' to what Homi Bhabha, the postcolonial cultural studies theorist, has called the 'unhomely': "The recesses of the domestic space become sites for history's most intricate invasions. In that displacement, the borders between home and world become confused; and uncannily, the private and public become part of each other, forcing upon us a vision that is as divided as it is disorienting"[19]. Bhabha further adds: "The unhomely moment relates the traumatic ambivalences of a personal, psychic history to the wider disjunctions of political existence"[20]. The cosmonaut-protagonist of *The Mark of Cassandra* rejects the planet, with both its systems of advanced capitalism (USA) and socialism (the erstwhile USSR), and chooses to live his last days in space, before he steps out of the space-station to sure death in the cosmos. In this Aitmatov's hero willfully 'dehomes' himself. From the '60s onwards, with the publication of *Mother's Field*, Aitmatov's works posed the 'home' as his central aesthetic category. However problem-ridden or threatened the home was, its relationship to its locality, its neighbourhood, the nation, the inter-nation was always portrayed. In the works of the '90s, the home is no longer the central aesthetic or ideological category. In the novella *The White Cloud of Genghiz Khan*, the self-censored section of the novel *And the Day Lasts Longer Than a Century*, the old Chinese servant takes her mistress' child, born of forbidden love, and goes into the steppes, after her mistress and her lover are executed by Genghiz Khan. In a contemporary narrative running parallel to this legend, the protagonist imprisoned by Stalin's henchmen, knows he will never return home again. He sees his home for the last time as he is being taken away in a train. The image of the home of being within reach, and yet

19. *The Location of Culture*, Homi K. Bhabha, Routledge, London, 2003, p. 9.
20. Ibid., p. 11.

unattainable, or a home that is lost in the nomadic life foisted by Genghis Khan, is very poignantly captured in this novella. The play, *Night of Remembrances*, written with the Kazakh writer, Mukhtar Shakhanov, addresses the question that is elections to the state and the people who will inhabit this state in the context of globalisation.

It is *The Mark of Cassandra*, however, that gives the fullest and most sustained elaboration of Aitmatov's political and aesthetic vision. In this work, he portrays the negative features of both the important political systems of the XX century, advanced capitalism and socialism. He relativises both the political systems; neither comes out as better than the other. There is no grand narrative ideologically. Although he is close to a postmodernist sensibility vis-a-vis the theme in this novel, aesthetically, he can be categorized as a postrealist for he adopts a mode that still relates to realism. Since modernism was never part of his aesthetic agenda, he did not and could not move into postmodernism. In an interview in 1997, he states that he does not want to now negate socialist realism: ". . . it played a positive role in the development of many national literatures. Now these literatures are independent; they have to live in the general environment of world literature"[21].

It is also of interest that Aitmatov uses science fiction not in a futuristic sense, but in the sense of a future time-frame that has somehow mingled with the present and the past. The time-frames are palimpsestic creating an uneasy feel of science-fiction in our midst, shorn of temporal distance. His use of science-fiction, like his use of oral traditions, gives his realism an added depth.

In his article the 'Semiotics of Culture and the Understanding of the Text', Lotman defines the following communicative moments of a text: (*a*) communication between the addresser and addressee, (*b*) between the auditorium and cultural tradition, (*c*) between the reader and his/her own self, (*d*) between the reader and the text and between the text and its cultural context. The collapse of the Soviet Union, led to a collapse of all the communicative moments outlined above for practicing cultural activists. It is to Aitmatov's credit that despite being 'dehomed', he found a way of metaphorising and theorizing this state

21. *Chingiz Aitmatov: Stat'i, Vystupleniya, Esse, Dialogi*, Sobraniye Sochinenij v 7 tomakh, Tom 7, Moskva,1998, p. 536.

and translating it into creative works. In the global context of world literature, a typology, in the Lotmanian sense, can be made of works of postcolonialism and postsocialism. Both movements represent the 'other than modernity' of their societies. Both speak of dehoming, but there is a difference: postcolonial texts, more often than not, have a notional sense of home, distanced/lost/imaginary.... Aitmatov's *The Mark of Cassandra* dispenses with even a notional sense of home. Filofei, the protagonist, rejects the very binary opposition of centre and periphery, by choosing the cosmos.... However, by keeping the larger framework in view, Aitmatov seems to refuse to withdraw into his 'local' framework, preferring instead a global framework.

In an interview in 1973 Chingiz Aitmatov had stated, "... 'being with one's own self' leads to ethnographism, having no creative value; in the worst case, it leads to a 'closedness', to an aesthetic nationalism.... The artist then sharply limits his possibilities, cutting off the road to generalisations about humanity, which is the highest and only aim of art"[22]. In this insistence on the 'other' for better self-realisation, Aitmatov seems to be echoing Bakhtin's views on cultural dialogism. It is in this belief that continuity is to be found in the work of this Kyrgyz writer, who has lived through several systemic transitions without giving up his inter-national outlook.

22. *Chingiz Aitmatov: Stat'i, Vystupleniya, Esse, Dialogi*, Sobraniye Sochinenij v 7 tomakh, Tom 7, Moskva, 1998, p. 251.

BIBLIOGRAPHY

Works by Chingiz Aitmatov

1952 Dziuyo

1953 Ashim

1954 Sipaichi, Belij Dozhd

1952 Soperniki, Na Bogare, Na Reke Baidamtal

1953 Litsom k Litsu, Jamilia

1954 Topolek Moi v Krasnoi Kosynke, Verblyuzhij Glaz

1955 Pervij Uchitel

1956 Materinskoe Pole, Krasnoe Yabloko

1957 Svidaniye so Synom

1958 Proshai Gulsary!

1959 Belij Parakhod/Posle Skazki

1960 Plach Pereletnei Ptitsy

1973 Voskhozhdeniye na Fudjiyamu (co-author)

1975 Ranniye Zhuravli

1977 Pegiy Pes, Begushij na Kraem More

1978 I Dolshe Veka Dlitsa Den/Burraniy Polustanok

1986 Plakha

1990 Beloe Oblako Chinghizkhana

1993 Oda Velichiyu Dukha

1995 Tavro Kassandry (Iz Eresei XX Veka)

1996 Noch Vospominaniya o Sokrate (co-author)

1996 Plach Okhotnika Nad Propastiyu

Books on Chingiz Aitmatov (Russian)

Abdyldazhan Akmataliev, *Chindiz Aitmatov i vzaimosvyazi literatury*, Bishkek, 1989.

Abdyldazhan Akmataliev, *Kosmos Aitmatova: Chelovek i Vselennaya*, Bishkek, 1995.

Abdyldazhan Akmataliev, *Plakha i chitateli*, Frunze, 1988.

Abdyldazhan Akmataliev, *Slovo ob Aitmatove*, Bishkek, 1991.

Abdyldazhan Akmataliev, *Znacheniye tvorcheskoi aktivnosti Chingiza Aitmatova v protsecce vzaimoobogosheniya natsionalnykh literatur*, Bishkek, 1994.

Arkady Khabishevich Isenov, *Psikhologizm sovremennoi prozy: Na materially tvorchestva Chingiza Aitmatova*, Alma-Ata, 1985.

Asanaliev Keshenbek, *Otkrytie cheloveka sovremennosti*, Frunze, 1968.

Gennady Sadyrovixch Bazarov, *Prikosnoveniye k lichnosti*, Frunze, 1984.

Georgij Dmitrievich Gachev, *Lyubov, chelovek, epokha: Rassuzhdeniya o povesti Jamiliya*, Moscow, 1965.

G. Gachev, *Chingiz Aitmatov I mirovaya literature*, Frunze, 1982.

Georgy Dmitrievich Gachev, *Chingiz Aitmatov*, Frunze, 1989.

Ilimkhan Djhumakanovna Lailieva, *Traditsii russkoi klassicheskoi i mirovoi literatury v Kirgizskoi proze*, Frunze, 1988.

K. Abdyldabekov (ed.), *Chingiz Aitmatov: Stati I retsenzii o evo tvorchestve*, Frunze, 1966.

Leonid Fyodorovich Stroilev, *Tvorchestvo Chingiza Aitmatova v zapadno-evropeiskoi kritike*, Frunze, 1988.

Levon Mkrtichevich Mkrtchyan, *Shepotka sloi na Armyanskoi zemle: O Chingize Aitmatove*, Erevan, 1988.

Mikhail Lukyanovich Seliverstov, *Otkroveniya Lyubvi*, Frunze, 1966.

N. M. Dmitrieva, *Problemy mnogonatsuiionalnoi sovetskoi prozy*, Saratov, 1975.

Nina Maksimovna Dmitrieva, *Aktualnie problemy mnogonatsionalnoi sovetskoi prozy*, Kalinin, 1981.

Nina Vasilievna Gasheva, *Vzaimodeistvie natsionalnykh literature XX veka*, Perm, 1983.

Pariza Mansurovna Mirza-Akhmedova, *Natsionalnaya epicheskaya traditsia v tvorchestve Chingiza Aitmatova*, Tashkent, 1980.

Pavel Evgenievich Glinkin, *Chingiz Aitmatov*, Leningrad, 1968.

Rustam Rakhmanaliev, *Chinghiz Aitmatov—Knigi i chitatel: Opyt konkretno-cotsiologicheskovo issledovaniya*, Frunze, 1988.

Tatyana Timofeevna Davydova, *Sovetskaya Kirgizskaya povest*, Frunze, 1989.

V. K. Mombekov, *Izucheniye povesti Aitmatova 'Pervij Uchitel'*, Frunze, 1967.

Viktor Grigorievich Levchenko, *Chingiz Aitmatov: Problemy petiki, zhanra, stilya*, Moscow, 1983.

Vladimir Fyodorovich Korkin, *Cheloveku o cheloveke*, Frunze, 1974.

Vladimir Ilych Voronov, *Chingiz Aitmatov: Ocherk tvorchestvo*, Moscow, 1976.

Articles (Russian)

Vladimir Tuchkov, *Chingiz Aitmatov kak zerkalo russkoi mechty*, Russkij Zhurnal, 21 April, 1999.

Interview (Russian)

Igor Izgarshev, *Chingiz Aitmatov: Shastlivij chelovek*, Argumenty I Fakty, 21 October, 1998.

Books on Chingiz Aitmatov (English)

Joseph P. Mozur, *The Parables From the Past: The Prose Fiction of Chingiz Aitmatov*, Pittsburgh, University of Pittsburgh Press, 1995.

Nina Kolesnikoff, *Myth in the Works of Chingiz Aitmatov,* in *New Directions in Soviet Literature*, Sheelagh Duffin Graham (ed.), N.Y., St. Martin's Press, 1990.

V. Novikov, *Chingiz Aitmatov*, Moscow, Raduga, 1987.

Articles on Chingiz Aitmatov (English)

Anthony Olcott, *What Faith in God-Contemporary?: Chingiz Aitmatov's Plakha*, Slavic Review 49 (1990)pp. 213-226.

Boris Shusteff, *Jewish Mankurts?* http://www.freeman.org

Encyclopaedia of Soviet Writers, Entry on Chingiz Aitmatov, SovLit.com

Gary L. Browning, Thomas F. Rogers, *Chingiz Aitmatov's The Executioner's Block: Through Dreams a Confrontation With Existential Good and Evil*, The Russian Review 51 (January 1992), pp. 72-83.

Halim Kara, *Chingiz Aitmatov: A Captive Mind,* Fourth Annual Central Eurasian Studies Conference, Indiana University, Feb. 8th, 1997.

Iraj Bashiri, *The Art of Chingiz Aitmatov's Stories*, 1991.

James Woodward, *Chingiz Aitmatov's Second Novel*, The Slavonic and East European Review, 69, (April 1991), pp. 201-220.

Joseph P. Mozur, *Doffing 'Mankurt's Cap': Chingiz Aitmatov's The Day Lasts More Than a Century and the Turkic National Heritage*, The Carl Beck Papers in Russian and East European Studies, University of Pittsburgh, Center for Russian and east European studies, No. 605, 1987.

Katerina Clark, *The Mutability of the Canon: Socialist Realism and Chingiz Aitmatov's I Dolshe Veka Dlitsa Den*, Slavic Review, 43 (Winter 1984), pp. 573-583.

Rita Pittman, *Chingiz Aitmatov's Plakha: Novel in the Time of Change*, The

Slavonic and East European Review, 66, (July 1988), pp. 357-379.

Stewart Paton, *Chingiz Aitmatov's First Novel: A New Departure*?, The Slavonic and East European Review, 42 (October 1984), pp. 496-510.

Z. A. Zhukov-Breschinsky, *Aitmatov Chingiz* in The Modern Encyclopaedia of Russian and Soviet Literatures, Vol. I, Harry B. Weber (ed.), Florida, Academic International Press, 1979, pp. 56-63.

Interview (English)

The Truth on Mount Fuji, Interview with Chingiz Aitmatov by Latika Padgaonkar, Pioneer, 11 December, 1997.

SELECTED ADAPTATIONS OF AITMATOV'S WORKS

Film	'Jamilia'	I. Poplavskaya
Opera	'Jamilia'	Composer Raukhberger
Operetta	'Krai Tyulpanov' Based on motifs from *Topolek...*	Rudyansky
Ballet	'Asel' Based on motifs from *Topolek...*	Bolshoi Theatre
Film	'Echo Lyubvi' Based on *Na Reke Baidamtal*	
Film	'Krasnoe Yabloko'	Tolomush Okeev
Telefilm	'Arman' Based on *Cvidaniye s Synom*	
Film	'Znoi' Based on *Verblyuzhij Glaz*	Larissa Shepitko
Film	'Pervij Uchitel'	Andrei Mikhalkov-Konchalovsky
Play	'Materinskoe Pole'	Adapted by many theatres
Opera	'Mat' based on *Materinskoe Pole*	Composers A. Maldybaev, V. Vlasov
Film	'Beg Inokhodtsa' Based on *Proshai Gulsary*	S. Urusevsky
Composition for Stage in 2 parts	'Materinskoe Pole'	V. L'vov Anokhin (M. Otdeleniye Rasprostraneniya Dramaticheskikh Proizvedeniyij)
Film	'Belij Parakhod'	Bolotbek Shamsiev
Film	'Voskhozhdeniye na Fudjiyamu'	Bolotbek Shamsiev

INDEX

A Night of Remembrances, 14, 46, 51, 74, 77, 96
Abdykalykov Aktan, 24
Adorno T., 91
Afghanistan, 25
Aitmatov Roza, 54–55
Aitmatov Turekul 54–55
Akhmatova Anna, 91
Al-Farabi, 72
Alma-Aty, 46
And the Day Lasts Longer Than a Century, 11–12, 17, 34, 56, 66, 96
Apollo, 27
Aragon Louis, 9
Armenia, 25
Asia, 48, 50, 62, 67, 72
Azerbaijan, 25

Bakhtin Mikhail, 57, 58, 81, 84, 97
Balasaguni, 72
Benjamin Walter, 91
Berkeley Bishop, 57
Bhabha Homi, 40, 95
Bogdanov A., 86
Brecht Bertolt, 91
Brussels, 10
Bukhara, 48
Bulgakov Mikhail, 92–93

Camus Albert, 40
Cassandra, 27, 28, 29
Central Asia, 10, 18, 43, 49–50, 62, 67, 69, 72–74
China, 47–48, 50
Communism, 71–72
Contramodernity, 92
Critical insider, 13
Crusades, 63

De Certeau Michel, 37-38
De Saussure Ferdinand, 81–82, 84
Deleuze Gilles and Guattari Felix, 42, 56, 79
Derrida Jacques, 69
Dialogues at Ikeda's Campfire, 53
Doktorova Larissa, 67, 78
Dostoevsky, 34, 76; *Crime and Punishment*, 20; Raskolnikov, 34; Karamazov Ivan, 34

Dzuiyo, the Newsboy, 12

Europe, 19, 49, 92
European readers, 24

Farewell, Gulsary!, 10–12, 35, 79, 90
Fedotov A., 12, 71

Gachev G., 85, 87
Galilei Galileo, 57, 60
Gorky Maxim, 88

Hitler, 25, 49
Hume David, 57

Ikeda Daisaku, 53, 55, 63–65

Jameson Frederic, 72
Jamilia, 9, 12, 85, 87

Kafka Franz, 92-93
Kapustin Mikhail, 89
Kazakhstan, 12, 16, 46, 72
Khan Genghis, 18–20, 22, 47–50, 63, 96
Khayyam, 72
Khazanov Anatoly, 50–51
Khrushchev Nikita, 54
Khwarazm, 48
Korea, 47
Korkin Vladimir, 39, 42, 64
Kyrgyz national identity, 15, 49, 51

Lem Stanislas, 34
Lipovetsky and Leiderman, 43, 75–77
Literary Kirgizstan, 9
Lotman Yuri, 81–83, 89, 96
Lowe Robert, 15–16, 50
Lukacs Georg, 91
Lyotard Francois, 70–71, 73

Manas, 49–50, 86
Mankurtism, 65–66; legends of the mankurts, 21
Master and Margarita, 93
Meeting With the Son, 12
Modernism, 75, 90–91
Mother's Field, 11, 88, 95

Narod, 65, 69

Otrar, 47–48
Outsider, 40

Pasternak Boris, 91
Perestroika, 14, 17
Piebald Dog Running on the Seashore, 12
Plato, 57
Plisetsky M., 86
Pomerants G., 39
Postmodernism, 70, 72, 75-76
Postrealism, 52, 74–77
Pravda, 9, 54

Realism, 11–12, 75–78, 85, 90–92
Red Apple, 12
Renaissance Asian, 62, 72
Renaissance European, 62
Rushdie Salman, 25, 31
Russell Bertrand, 57
Russia, 11–12, 30–32, 41, 47–48, 63, 71

Sahni Kalpana, 35
Sakharov, 25, 36–37
Samizdat, 17, 91
Science fiction, 34–35, 96
Shakhanov Mukhtar, 14, 46, 53–55, 61, 63, 72, 96
Siberia, 18
Socialist realism, 13, 71, 77–79, 89, 90–91
Socrates, 56–57; Socratic dialogues 57–58
Solaris, 35

Soviet Union, 10, 14–15, 43, 50, 69, 71, 91, 94
Stalin, 12, 25, 49; Stalinism, 35, 70
Strugatsky Arkady and Boris, 34

Talas Valley, 9
Tamizdat, 17, 91
Taraz, 48
Tarkovsky Andrei, 35
The Hunter's Lament, 14, 53–54, 64, 68, 74
The Mark of Cassandra, 12, 14, 23–25, 33, 35–36, 38–41, 74, 77, 79, 95–97
The Trial, 92–93
The White Cloud of Chingiz Khan, 14, 17, 56, 77, 95
The White Steamship, 11, 35, 79

Ulan Bator, 50
USA, 30–32, 41, 44–45
Uzbekistan, 16
We, 34

Zametki o Sebe, 68
Zamyatin Evgeny, 34